strategic
TEAMS and
DEVELOPMENT

The FieldBook for
People Making Strategy Happen

STRATEGIC TEAMS AND DEVELOPMENT

The FieldBook for
People Making Strategy Happen

Daniel Wolf

Dewar Sloan
Consultants and Advisors to Management

dsb Publishing

Published by dsb Publishing
Administrative Offices:
P.O. Box 331
Traverse City, MI 49685-0331

ISBN 13: 978-0-9791300-3-8
Library of Congress Control Number: 2019904918
Printed in the United States
10 9 8 7 6 5 4 3 2 1
Development by Team SC/24

Project Manager, Brooke Felger
SC/24 Development, Dana Boomer

Comments and Reflections

"Teams are essential when it comes to making strategy happen – and their role has become even more important in our age of agility and collaboration. Daniel Wolf's FieldBook casts well-curated, comprehensive, and refreshingly multidisciplinary lenses on the many dimensions that contribute to the success of teams. A great source for anybody who wants to drive change."

Roland Deiser, *Center for the Future of Organization at Drucker School of Management*

*"**Strategic Teams and Development** is a powerful framework for connecting strategy, talent and culture. Wolf has carefully woven the keys to collaboration and accountability into this most useful and practical FieldBook."*

Jon Gordon, *Bestselling Author of THE POWER OF POSITIVE LEADERSHIP*

"Daniel Wolf provides critical insights on the integration of culture, talent, and Strategic Teams, the essential elements for driving organizational growth, performance and change."

Tim Myers, *Van Andel Institute*

"Of all that fuels teams – creativity has the potential to be a driving force. In the communication business, creativity becomes the energy that builds bridges, explores new frontiers and helps teams reach their full potential. Daniel Wolf gets that completely. His assessment of creative capital, and the work of connecting teams to advance the enterprise is spot on."

Jake Lestan, *DDB Chicago*

"Here is a very practical approach to the construction and development of effective teams. As a people manager, I'm always looking for tips and strategies to improve how our teams function. Daniel Wolf provides a wealth of good advice around the issues that advance/constrain team effectiveness and performance. He provides a vivid picture for team development and sustenance."

Scott Hanton, **PhD**, *Intertek*

"The success of leading a business has progressively become more challenging. Daniel Wolf captures the essentials that leaders need to nurture their organization to thrive by understanding and effectively executing strategy, aligned with culture and a sound leadership approach."

Andy Blanchard, *Syntron Material Handling*

*"**Strategic Teams and Development** resonates on many levels. Building and supporting the kind of talent that drives growth, performance and change is one of the key tasks of senior leaders, and leaders at every level of the enterprise. This is critical to execution, near-term/long-term success."*

Roch Lambert, *Curt Manufacturing Group*

"Leadership is built on self-awareness and the questions we ask ourselves. Are we prepared, focused, ready, engaged, capable, and resolved? **Strategic Teams and Development** *is a very well-crafted framework for guiding thoughtful, motivated leaders across the strategic and cultural journey of business evolution, both near-term and long-term."*

Dr. Marshall Goldsmith, *Bestselling Author of TRIGGERS and other books, Executive Coach*

"Daniel Wolf has brought together the key pieces of the "making strategy happen" puzzle - in a practical and value-focused manner. The importance of Strategic Teams in today's rapidly evolving business environment cannot be overstated. This book establishes a terrific frame of reference for those who are working to execute the organization's essential projects."

Sean Healy, *Amazon*

"Today's supply chain models demand individuals and teams that have greater intimacy with key stakeholders, understanding that success comes from consistent performance, continuous improvement and organizational agility, without compromising individual, team or enterprise core values. This book pulls no punches on the factors that enable individuals and teams to consistently deliver. Very relevant to leaders at every stakeholder level."

John Evans, *Ingersoll Rand*

"Strategic Teams and Development *provides the bridge for getting the right people into sync on teams that execute plans and make progress on business development work at every level. Daniel Wolf makes it clear that teams are the agents of making strategy happen. And a bonus, great questions throughout the book. And, another bonus, great references for ongoing team development. Highly useful for every day thought and behavior, valuable."*

Tamara Steffens, *Microsoft*

*"***Strategic Teams and Development** *brings to life a critical topic which is all too often reserved for academia - strategy integration and execution. The vast array of references and resources provided in the FieldBook make it very useful to those of us that face the challenge of making strategy happen every day. But the overall focus on creating new strategic and economic value is what comes through as paramount."*

Jeff McMullen, *LNS America*

"I highly recommend **Strategic Teams and Development** *to anyone actively thinking about talent and how it relates to strategy and culture. This FieldBook meets a company where it is at any given time, and provides specific frameworks that fit into a wide range of business systems and resources. This new book from Daniel Wolf will be worth your time."*

James Lane, *RedBank Advisors*

*"The future of organizations depends on dedicated experts, well-engaged in the processes of learning with an urgent focus on next horizon skills, capacities and a clear, full sense of purpose. **Strategic Teams and Development** raises the bar on matching talent and culture."*

David Blake, Co-Author of THE EXPERTISE ECONOMY

*"Effective collaboration at the strategic level depends on individuals and enterprise teams who can bring their expertise, perspective, energy and experience to the table in ways that advance the cause of something greater. **Strategic Teams and Development** provides resources for those of us who are working to build new frontiers of service, value and opportunity for our stakeholders."*

Emma Schwartz, Medical Center of the Americas

*"**Strategic Teams and Development** - a FieldBook essential for building cohesive, engaged and highly effective teams. This FieldBook provides a sustainable framework for building teams and results that are quantifiable. By applying the framework we have effectively grown from individuals into a highly effective team that applies its collective intelligence and energy into delivering results that align with the Strategic Agenda of our organization."*

Kate Wolstenholme, Medtronic

*"Every successful organization is built on strong and effective teams. Daniel Wolf's new book, **Strategic Teams and Development**, is an invaluable FieldBook that explains in detail how to create and nurture effective work teams throughout your organization."*

Eric Nee, Stanford Social Innovation Review

"The work of product development depends on teams of people whose diverse skills and insights serve to shape concepts, design options, frame solutions and advance value. This book gathers the essence of what makes teams successful, in highly disciplined, yet practical terms, providing clear and consistent perspectives. The references provided in each section are valuable by themselves."

David Harris, DHA Design Management Group

"There is a broadly human, perhaps spiritual track in this FieldBook, one that starts with respect for people, service and communication. Relationship Competency, within Strategic Teams, is critical for any organization to achieve superior results. This is not all soft-side though, as Wolf gets right after the factors that make the team greater than the sum of its individual parts."

Tom Livengood, Leadership Enhancement

"Throughout my career, I have depended on strong, effective teamwork to successfully implement our organizational strategy and deliver on our mission. This FieldBook provides a practical but elegant guide to developing high-performing teams that drive effective outcomes."

Dr. Helene Gayle, The Chicago Community Trust

"The value of a business is a function of how well the financial capital and the intellectual capital are managed by the human capital. You better get the human capital right. My colleague Daniel Wolf has assembled the pieces of the puzzle with strategy, talent and culture in a practical manner."

David Bookbinder, Author of THE NEW ROI: RETURN ON INDIVIDUALS

"This FieldBook is a bold stroke for those of us who navigate the challenges of healthcare change, innovation, value and outcomes. The author's framework for strategy is bolted to a powerful view of the Talent Blocks and Beams to address the staffing and leadership of critical teams. These ideas will settle well in the journey of healthcare leaders everywhere, at every level."

Ryan Armbruster, University of Minnesota

"The success of any business is directly linked to the investment and development of the people who make up the teams that drive strategic execution. This book reveals a thorough understanding of the details and actions involved in developing teams and the culture required to successfully deliver results and move the company forward."

Dave Gillrie, Blount International

"It isn't news that it is much easier to formulate strategy than to actually execute it. This innovative book is like a do-it-yourself cookbook, where many key ingredients and tools for making wonderful meals are included as important resources for the reader to stimulate exploration and thoughtful, coordinated action. The concepts of Talent Blocks and Beams are used as ground on which to build and use influence to shape everyday thinking and behavior to create effective Strategic Teams."

Allan Cohen, Co-Author of INFLUENCE WITHOUT AUTHORITY, Babson College

"**Strategic Teams and Development** is a fresh and long-needed perspective on strategy and the talent that makes things happen across the business landscape. The author has put together a complete and dynamic view of the range of talent that enables multi-functional teams to perform, evolve, adapt and sustain progress. This is one terrific resource for business growth and change leaders. All the right questions, and a great framework for answering those questions."

Chris M. Jones, Adobe

"Strategy is a system for making things happen, for managing progress, defending a cause, advancing the mission. My friend and colleague, Daniel Wolf, reflects clearly on the alignment of strategy, talent, culture and the need to adapt - in systemic ways - to the challenges we face. **Strategic Teams and Development** is a very solid resource, with broad applications for teams of people in every endeavor, every journey, great and small."

Brad Graft, Executive, U.S. Marine Officer, Author of BROTHERHOOD OF THE MAMLUKS

Contents

PART TWO
Individual and Team Capacity

PART THREE
Moving Strategic Teams Ahead

Foreword

Everyone has a stake in workforce teams and development. Strategic teams in one form or another have become the organizational unit for making things happen. Teams are practical structures that design and execute, frame options and decisions, match risks and routes, adapt and persist. Teams acquire, arrange and apply knowledge. They exchange perspective and points of judgment. Teams shape cultures that are sensitive, adaptive and powerful.

In my experience and tenure, the most effective teams are collections of talented people, working together with discipline, a culture of trust and shared purpose, with a practical sense of how to get things done. The most effective teams are not perfect, but most have learned to perform by gathering their personal and collective abilities together for the cause. People on strong teams work effectively, collectively.

When we look at the basic talent set of an individual, there are many attributes we can observe or presume. Some people are good planners and others are good at matters of implementation. Some people have a knack for problem solving and others are good with communication work. Some people are focused on tomorrow; others have today clocked by the hour. The diverse talents of people provide the starting point for developing teams that are capable, motivated, intentional, persistent and focused.

Team development seldom takes place in a void, however. Effective teams are built from individuals with the general capacity and competence to work together on projects and programs. Perhaps that work is tied to operating practices and compliance. Or maybe that work is geared to discovery and forward planning. The general capacity and competence of a team is something that we think about by roles and functions, goals and purpose. What do we want our teams to accomplish? What do we want our teams to become? What stands in our way, and how do we adapt and move forward? These questions guide our sense of purpose in Strategic Teams, their development, and how they drive the creation of value.

The developmental journey of teams requires exposure, learning, practice, experience, review, more practice, leadership and reflection, and more learning. Effective teams are continuous improvement sparks, with a bias for ongoing Learning and Development. That bias helps engage people in the everyday thought and behavior that drives results and forges the communal presence and leadership of talented people. The road to excellence.

My view of teams has evolved over the years. Many of the ideas in this FieldBook resonate deeply with me, and here are a few that stand out as ongoing principles that make a big difference. Individuals bring unique gifts and interests to teams; our efforts should bring out the best in people in the context of the work and charter of the team. The work itself conditions the team to grow, perform, deliver and serve; our development efforts should "capture" and "ratchet" our teams and their capacity for growth, performance and change.

Teams are communal structures, with specific competence and culture as their base for power and influence. Our efforts should guide the curation of that power for positive impact and stewardship. Teams are nurtured and supported in the currency of trust; our efforts should concentrate on trust, confidence, energy and the cohesion of the team.

There are many kinds of teams. There are many kinds of people, with the individual talent that could bring great value to different kinds of teams. This FieldBook provides a great perspective, a framework and the right vocabulary to develop individual talent and team effectiveness in different settings. I know this is the way forward, with Strategic Teams. I also know that the work of building teams and keeping them on track is not easy. Some might suggest that the development of teams that drive an organization captures the nature of culture through practice. That has great appeal to me.

Christopher Wollam

Austin, Texas
06.30.2019

Preface

This FieldBook has origins that trace back a couple of decades. We looked at the skill sets of our project teams and the nature of their work together for ideas that would move the needle on coverage, speed and results. We drew some insights from the available research on human development, cognitive differences, behavioral patterns, group communication, systems management and strategic leadership. We cooked up a few models that might explain how individuals work, and how teams are formed and how they prosper.

We looked at the different kinds of talent, different forms of interaction, different tasks, challenges and roles. We assigned individuals with different talents to teams with different structures, goals and resources. Along the way, we exchanged ideas about effective teams, team challenges and team development with hundreds of organizations, across many sectors, and across borders. We drew heavily from common sense and human experience. We explored the essence of teams, the relevance of team attitudes, the depth and range of team skills, the acumen of team members, the cohesion of teams, the motives of teams and the pathways, speed, power, and processes of teams.

We know that people grow up in this world with different biological, environmental and situational factors that shape their talent and mindset. Surely part of our approach to life in this world is just a matter of who we are and how we mature, in the settings where we were nurtured and challenged. What we learn along the way informs how we work together and what we bring to the collective and communal value of teams.

What talent we bring to our respective teams is part innate, part learned. The focus of this FieldBook is the definition and connection of individual and team talent in the context of **making strategy happen**. We know that organizations of all stripes experience some challenges in project integration and strategy execution. The capacity and competence of teams can be gauged in many ways, and we know from broad experience that teams are effective "talent blenders" if they are well developed and built to operate well. That guidance sets people on the path to maturity, responding to strategic challenges.

Strategic Teams and Value-Added

Teams are, in essence, structures that enable and support the strategy of organizations. Teams, and the individuals who comprise them, are working mechanisms that engage and support strategy direction, integration and execution. The designation, charters and dispersion of teams are key leadership and management tasks. Organizations direct and staff teams to become **the effective agents of making strategy happen**, at every level, in every setting and situation. That makes this platform for **Strategic Teams and Development** so relevant to the Strategic Agenda of the contemporary organization ... Consider that Strategic Teams:

- **Are Part of Forward Planning**
  - *Dealing wisely with near-term and long-term*

- **Are Part of Decision Making**
  - *Discerning key decision criteria and consequences*

- **Are Part of Risk Management**
  - *Anticipating, managing, dealing with risk factors*

- **Are Part of Problem Solving**
  - *Sensing the nature of problems and alternatives*

- **Are Part of Value Creation**
  - *Scoping both economic and strategic value*

There are textbooks and story books about teams and talent, competence and capacity, strategy and structure, focus and impact. This is a **practical FieldBook**, and our purpose is the **greater engagement of talented people in well-developed Strategic Teams, for results, for growth, performance and change, for sustenance and value-added.**

Daniel Wolf

Traverse City, Michigan
06.30.2019

Strategic Teams and Competence

The research on cognitive, functional, emotional and behavioral development provides ample references to the different kinds of capacity and competence that people bring to teams. We based this FieldBook on a working framework that recognizes individual and collective talent that reflect in six areas of Strategic Team interaction:

- ***Technical Competence, Capacity, Engagement***
  - *Knowledge bases; subject matter expertise*

- ***Analytic Competence, Capacity, Engagement***
  - *Data sense, patterns, signals, markers*

- ***Creative Competence, Capacity, Engagement***
  - *New ideas, points of view, approaches*

- ***Resource Competence, Capacity, Engagement***
  - *Getting more from available resources*

- ***Solution Competence, Capacity, Engagement***
  - *Problem recognition and paths to resolution*

- ***Relational Competence, Capacity, Engagement***
  - *Engaging people to adapt and persevere*

Some organizations depend on teams that are geared to policy compliance, order, steady and deliberate practice. Some organizations depend on their teams to discern and navigate complex situations and challenges with moving targets. Some organizations operate with continuous attention to the new/next and the novel connection of ideas, processes and forms. Some organizations need constant attention to the improvement of processes and standards, systems and operations. **Each of these patterns prescribes a Strategic Team, with talent that reflects the "work-to-be-done" by the team.   But there is more.**

Strategic Teams and Confidence

Our experience with the development and deployment of teams at every level helps shape a view about confidence as well. This also derives from cognitive, functional, emotional and behavioral factors that come together in such basic ideas as trust, energy and power. Strategic Teams depend on:

- ***Information Exchanges***
  - *and confidence in the integrity of know-how*

- ***Personal and Interpersonal Relationships***
  - *and confidence in the work and support of others*

- ***Direction and Leadership Decisions***
  - *and confidence in the focus and choices that are made*

- ***Experience and Resources***
  - *and confidence in the capacity to deliver what counts*

- ***Attitudes and Mindsets***
  - *and confidence in the team's readiness and preparedness*

- ***Communal Engagement***
  - *and confidence in the team itself, the pride factor*

Add some determination, tap some inner faith and passion for the cause. Add some respect, draw some wisdom and sense of perspective. Add some passion, gather some collective grasp of the work to be done and purpose to serve, an outcome to assume. Generate a confident picture of Strategic Team value. Advance a confident team into the work of making strategy happen. Adapt to a broad range of challenging conditions and new challenges without losing force or cadence. Yes, Strategic Teams are built and sustained with confidence, and sometimes confidence alone.

Dedication, True Leadership

Steve Krakoff was a thoughtful executive and a generous contributor to our discussions on strategic leadership. His insights on people, organizations and policy are reflected in this FieldBook. Steve was active in our early work on strategy direction, integration and execution. He was always there for a good debate on issues that shape strategy options for management and governance. He brought perspective and common sense.

Steve was also a great personal and professional friend, a true, faithful, distance-bridging fellow. We shared business, political, cultural, social, and spiritual interests. We also shared the power of a really good [private] joke, the beauty of a well-crafted Limerick, and metaphors that connect old and new ideas. Always bright and hopeful. Skilled and intense. Always willing and giving, open to influence. The good man, the good servant.

Dedication, Teams Everywhere

This FieldBook reflects on a lot of great work by people who serve on teams in business, government, education, research, healthcare, family systems, military service, the performing arts and culture, sports, entertainment, religion, conservation, farming, construction and technology. Wherever people come together to serve with purpose and advance a cause, wherever they lead themselves and each other in some kind of Strategic Agenda for growth, performance and change, wherever they endeavor to bring out the best in others - we give them our deepest respect.

06.30.2019

Advancement, Teams Everywhere

This FieldBook is part of a teams and development resource that serves many organizational needs. Variations on the content of this FieldBook have been designed to commission new teams, restructure existing teams, redirect teams in extended action and assignments, pull operational teams together, direct joint-team ventures and other tasks. Broad sections of this FieldBook have also been kept as proprietary manuals for organizational Learning and Development, Executive Development, Task-Forward Leadership, Transformation Programs and a range of functional new product/service programs.

Prologue

We settled the main themes of strategy into a framework for growth, performance and change about a decade ago. This framework has become a platform of sorts, shaping the everyday thought and behavior of people who are charged with making strategy happen, which includes most people in most organizations. We call this the **Strategic Agenda** …

Strategy direction is about focus and choices. Organizations focus on priorities and prerogatives based on their Natural Goals and the conditions of the marketplace and the organization. Direction is where things are headed in order to create and sustain value.

Strategy integration is about systems and resources, capital and networks, processes and structures. Strategy integration is the "stage house" in which the intentions and capacities of the organization come together, with competence, mindset, culture and confidence.

Strategy execution is about action and impact. People take action in ways that shape impact; they are active learners and leaders, and active "everyday agents" of the organization's Strategic Agenda. Execution blends strategic mission and human passion.

Prepared and Resolved: the Strategic Agenda

This FieldBook is a working companion to **Prepared and Resolved**, a book that explores the practical nature of strategy leadership and management. **Prepared and Resolved** served to outline the Strategic Agenda for growth, performance and change. The applications of that book have evolved as the Learning and Development platform reflected in this FieldBook.

Natural Goals, Intentions

For most organizations, the measures of success come down to themes and markers that are tied to what we have called the **Four Natural Goals.** In every purpose, vision and mission statement of substance, these Natural Goals tie to value creation and sustenance with:

Customer Connections	Competitive Advantage	Economic Performance	Corporate Stewardship

- Every organization has **customer connections**. They include market and channel partners, as well as investors and development partners, stakeholders of all manner and type that depend on the people of the organization to make things work.

- Every organization has some basis for **competitive advantage**, the elements that give it some kind of comparative edge, a difference, an approach to the marketplace that is somehow better and more relevant to needs, interests, challenges and goals.

- Every organization depends on positive **economic performance**, the sound use of assets and capital, the effective management of critical resources, the sustenance of people, systems and assets, and the management of revenue, expenses and resources.

- Every organization practices some kind of **corporate stewardship**, the trusted care of scarce resources, the public good, the moral good and the private good that merge together in enterprise responsibility. Corporate stewardship is ballast for the enterprise.

When Strategic Teams master their purpose, these Natural Goals serve as the True North, the guidance system for what matters, and why, for whomever. Most organizations have performance gauges that track conditions and progress relative to key indicators. These provide markers that match different dimensions of the Four Natural Goals.

CONSIDER:
[Play to Win, La Piana]
[Social Ecosystem and Ecology, Global Peter Drucker Forum]
[The Triple Bottom Line, Savitz and Weber]
[Good Company, Bassi, Frauenheim, McMurrer, and Costello]
[Innovation and Entrepreneurship, Drucker]

Getting Strategic Talent Engaged

Individuals and teams are the agents of the organization's Strategic Agenda. Better talent can be gauged in many ways, reflecting capacity and competence, knowledge and judgment, influence and perspective, discipline and confidence. Our premise is simple and natural: **people make strategy happen**, so the prerogatives of the organization should be geared to matching individuals and Strategic Teams to the work that shapes the creation of value.

Where we see highly-engaged teams at work, driving the organization's planning and decision making, there are several key indicators that deserve consideration:

Team Respect and Appreciation	**Interpersonal Trust and Effort**
Systems, Order and Arrangement	**Natural Forces of Collaboration**
Accountability and Commitment	**Consideration of Shared Influence**

Personal and communal engagement is a big deal for teams, and the evidence points to team engagement as an essential ingredient in organizations with a Strategic Agenda that makes sense and gets done. Much of this FieldBook focuses on guiding specific capacities at the individual level, matched in the collective power, energy and trust of teams.

CONSIDER:
[You Are the Team, Rogers]
[The Meaning Revolution, Kofman]
[The Leading Brain, Fabritius and Hagemann]
[20 Kinds of Teams, Dewar Sloan Working Paper, Wolf and Felger]

FieldBook and Focus

This FieldBook reflects 25+ years of research and planning experience. The general elements defined in this FieldBook have been shaped by ancient themes in organization and learning, along with modern themes in neuroscience and behavior. However, most of this FieldBook reflects the common sense of how individuals and teams bring together their capacity and competence and their "collective smarts" for making strategy happen.

FieldBook Approach

There are three parts of this FieldBook. **Part One** provides the background and rationale for **Strategic Teams and Development**, setting up the definitions and constructs of individual and team capacity, competence, the Strategic Agenda, maturity, connections and evolution.

Part Two provides a blueprint for each of six areas of team capacity and development based on essential Learning and Development themes. These include:

- *Technical Capacity and Competence ...*

- *Analytic Capacity and Competence ...*

- *Creative Capacity and Competence ...*

- *Resource Capacity and Competence ...*

- *Solution Capacity and Competence ...*

- *Relational Capacity and Competence ...*

Separate chapters cover each of these areas with a common outline of approach. Definitions are provided in a manner that serves a range of applications. These definitions also support cultural adaptation and change in different kinds of organizations.

Part Three was designed to reset the **Strategic Teams and Development** framework in terms that make the most sense for specific organizations - with people in different roles, with different gifts and focus firing-up **people making strategy happen**.

FieldBook Use and Comments

Strategic Teams and Development was written to help organizations prosper and advance with people who are well-engaged. With a FieldBook, our focus is on *practical* Leadership and Management, *practical* Learning and Development. There are many technical and academic ideas that are embedded in this platform, and the research and theory that support this FieldBook are the subject of discussion for those who have plenty of time for such matters. Here, however, are a few pointers for FieldBook usage and application:

- *This approach is **learning platform and technology agnostic**, and that means the owners can embrace this platform regardless of the enterprise systems, the Learning and Development system or the relationship systems in place. Further, it means that talent diagnostic and assessment systems will mesh well with the elements of **Strategic Teams and Development**, provided that talent management people understand the nature of the elements we've set in the definition of talent.*

- *This approach is **resource and culturally scalable**, and that means the owners can match this platform with small and large groups, across functions, project teams, business units, subsidiaries, ventures and acquisitions. It also means that this platform is well-suited to the Dual-Dynamic aspects of the organization's Strategic Agenda, taking care of today - while getting ready for tomorrow.*

- *This approach is **adaptive to mixed structures**, and that means across the spectrum of high bureaucracy to open organization models. Every enterprise can benefit from the **Strategic Teams and Development** platform. We have experience with this model in standard structures, blended structures, matrix organizations, lattice structures, start-ups, M&A integration, transitions, advanced development and innovation structures, paradox teams and transformation teams.*

- *This approach is **built for everyday progress and evolution**, and that means the organization can use these elements to embrace the tensions of growth, performance and change with confidence. It also means that teams can apply the elements of this FieldBook as autonomous efforts, as collective efforts, as disruptive efforts and as recovery efforts. Agile organizations are built with adaptive team assets and this FieldBook is geared to role-enabled personal learning networks, or environments.*

Questions, Everywhere

This FieldBook contains a wide range of questions. The intention here is to promote and exchange conversation and discernment. The intention is also to engage individuals and teams in the everyday thought and behavior that goes with making strategy happen. Serious thinking. Critical thinking. Comparative thinking. Reflective thinking. Constructive skepticism. Responsive behavior. Focused behavior. Comparative study. Credible analysis. The prospects for civil discourse, blended with common work to be done, balanced by the search for answers, truth, purpose and the impact of growth, performance and change.

References - Materials to Consider

This FieldBook also contains a wide range of general references that may provide subjects for further background study, or take-off points for Strategic Teams. These generally refer to broad ideas, published works or subjects that contribute to the concepts we're addressing. The end notes contain a range of expanded subject matter that supports the development of individual and team attributes, capabilities and resilience.

Further Comments on FieldBook Usage

Individual and small group users of this general platform may consider the elements of this FieldBook for specific applications and initiatives that can become part of the following:

- *Modular Learning and Development Programs*

- *Professional Development and Executive Development*

- *Personal Development, Leadership and Self-Governance*

- *Partnership Development and Collaborative Programs*

- *Individual Development, Coaching and Assessment*

- *Project Acceleration and Progress Management*

Strategic Teams and Development is a resource for individuals and organizations, and our intent with this FieldBook is to provide a practical, thorough guide to the processes and practices of effective Learning and Development. **People make strategy happen.**

PART 1

BACKGROUND AND CHALLENGES

*Teamwork is the ability to work together toward
a common vision ... the fuel that allows common people
to attain uncommon results.*

Andrew Carnegie

*Great things in business are never done by one person;
they're done by a team of people.*

Steve Jobs

*If you want to go quickly, go alone -
if you want to go far, go together.*

African Proverb

CHAPTER 01
INTRODUCTION

Strategy, Talent and Culture

People make strategy happen. For many of us, that may be a simple restatement of the obvious. People with the right talent and the capacity to work effectively with other people under different conditions are going to be successful in making strategy happen.

The everyday thought and behavior of individuals working in teams is what makes an organization more or less successful, near-term and long-term. This everyday thought and behavior forms in the cultures and subcultures of organizations, further reflecting:

- ***How We Communicate***
  - *Content, process, channels*

- ***How We Manage Knowledge***
  - *Developing, sorting, dispersing*

- ***How We Connect with One Another***
  - *Personal, collective, communal*

- ***How We Navigate Challenges***
  - *Attention, responding, adapting*

- ***How We Advance the Cause***
  - *Purpose, roadmap, energy*

What we value and why we focus on key elements of our work are essential as we deal with the journey of making strategy happen. This journey involves critical thought and behavior in forward planning, decision making, risk management and problem solving. People across the spans and structures of organizations choose to engage, or not, in these critical efforts. This is the journey of people who drive the creation of economic and strategic value.

CONSIDER:
[Talent is Never Enough, Maxwell]
[Talent is Overrated, Colvin]
[Power Score, Smart and Smart]
[Leadershift: Essential Changes Every Leader Must Embrace, Maxwell]

Why These Things Matter

Most organizations have some kind of strategic plan. Some of these are detailed and layered with direction, integration and execution elements. Some are framed in a "Dual-Dynamic" form which takes into account the evolutionary patterns of business development strategy.

> Dual-Dynamic Mindset and Strategy Means:
>
> • *Balancing Near-Term and Long-Term Challenges, Alternatives, Objectives, Relationships, Focus*
>
> • *Balancing Core Business Intentions with Adjacent Development Options, and Pathways*

What we've experienced over roughly three decades of work on strategy and governance is that individuals and teams quite often struggle with this work in strategy direction, integration and execution. And, based on our research and experience, the struggle is real:

- **Strategy Direction Means Focus and Choices**
  - *20% to 25% of organizations struggle with strategy direction*

- **Strategy Integration Means Priorities and Resources**
  - *65% to 70% of organizations struggle with strategy integration*

- **Strategy Execution Means Action and Impact**
  - *35% to 40% of organizations struggle with strategy execution*

The many challenges and nuances of strategy direction, integration and execution are covered in a wide range of strategy and governance sources. For this FieldBook, however, what matters is simply this ... getting talented people engaged in positive ways, with the right abilities and passions, settled in a culture of readiness and evolution for the work of making strategy happen. This applies in every organization, large and small.

CONSIDER:
[Dual-Dynamic Strategy: Research Notes, Wolf and Boomer]
[Finish Big; Small Giants, Burlingham]

Why and How This Makes a Difference

Individuals and teams are motivated, more or less, by their match of interests within the organization. This reflects their combined interests in the organization's:

- **Purpose, Focus, Intentions**
  - *The expression of mission and cause*

- **Mindset for Growth and Development**
  - *The expectation of advancement, evolution*

- **Approach to Leadership and Management**
  - *The inspiration and administration of effort*

- **Support for Making Things Happen**
  - *The resources and security for getting things done*

These are part of the culture and strategy "picture" that attracts employees, attaches team capacity, forges competencies, shapes Learning and Development and brings order and balance to the lives of people at every level of the enterprise.

Individuals and teams find their contentment and confidence in settings that encourage their purpose and value as part of the organization. They form the talent supply chains that drive competitive advantage and economic performance. They drive value creation.

CONSIDER:
[Alive at Work, Cable]
[Build an A Team, Johnson]
[Mindset, The New Psychology of Success, Dweck]
[Born to Build, Clifton, Badal]
[Triggers: Creating Behavior that Lasts, Goldsmith and Reiter]
[Why Firms Succeed, Kay]
[Growth Mindset Culture for Leadership Development, Dweck and Hogan]

Starting with the Strategic Agenda

Teams cannot be effective without a clear view of the organization's Strategic Agenda. Individuals and teams are agents of the Strategic Agenda, and therefore:

- *They need a complete and discerning view of what the organization stands for and where it's headed over time. Context, perspective.*

- *They need the organization's story on near-term/long-term priorities, goals and challenges. Past to present, and future.*

- *They need sharp practical sense of the organization's strategic direction – the mission command focus, and choices for development.*

- *They need a sense of perspective on the organization's strategy integration platform, with systems, processes, resources and cadence.*

- *They need a working framework for the organization's actions, throughputs and efforts that apply across strategy execution.*

The most effective teams are not just informed about strategy, they are immersed in the culture and mechanisms for the work of **people making strategy happen.**

CONSIDER:
[The Inevitable, Kelly]
[Play to Your Strengths, Mercer]
[Tasks of a Strategic Leader, Petraeus]
[Simple Rules, Sull and Eisenhardt]
[The Strategy Paradox, Raynor]
[Strategy: A History, Freedman]
[The Rise and Fall of Strategic Planning, Mintzberg]

The Strategic Agenda - Expanded

Most common concerns about strategic planning stem from the many disconnects that organizations experience with direction, integration and execution. In addition, strategy is adaptive by nature, and planning processes get bogged down by models that don't have a dynamic platform. The Strategic Agenda is an alternative to conventional strategic planning frameworks. It connects strategy direction, strategy integration and strategy execution in a practical and dynamic approach. Here is a general summary of a Strategic Agenda:

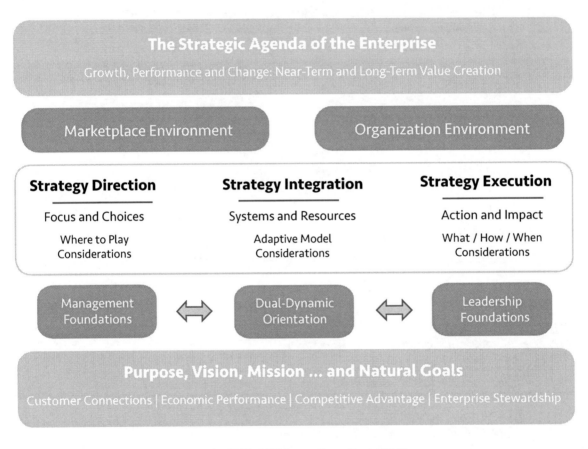

The Strategic Agenda of the Enterprise

Growth, Performance and Change: Near-Term and Long-Term Value Creation

Marketplace Environment

Organization Environment

Strategy Direction

Focus and Choices

Where to Play
Considerations

Strategy Integration

Systems and Resources

Adaptive Model
Considerations

Strategy Execution

Action and Impact

What / How / When
Considerations

Management Foundations ⟷ Dual-Dynamic Orientation ⟷ Leadership Foundations

Purpose, Vision, Mission ... and Natural Goals

Customer Connections | Economic Performance | Competitive Advantage | Enterprise Stewardship

Copyright, 2007 - 2019 Dewar Sloan, Daniel Wolf

The direction, integration and execution of strategy is a connected, adaptive stream of efforts and investments that advance the organization and create new value.

Exploring the Strategic Agenda Further

The leadership and management of Strategic Teams starts with an understanding of strategy as a framework for growth, performance and change. This framework serves to influence the plans and decisions that contribute to value creation. Most organizations exist to serve stakeholders and create sustainable value in one form or another. This may include:

- **Economic Value**
  - *Expressed in Terms of Revenue, Margins and Capital Teams*

- **Strategic Value**
  - *Expressed in Terms of Capacity, Systems and Market Position*

The Strategic Agenda is a framework that connects the essential themes, challenges, risks, behaviors and impact of strategy direction [focus and choices], strategy integration [priorities and resources], and strategy execution [action and impact] as a whole.

For individuals and teams, the broader strokes of the organization's Strategic Agenda provide the essential "why" of things, along with a general sense of the "who" that serve in responsible roles and functions, and the "what, how, when" of making strategy happen. That simple, and that complex. And that is how strategy, talent and culture emerge as the common factors in organizational growth, performance and change.

The **value proposition** of an organization is a statement that gathers many of the elements of the Strategic Agenda together. The general content of an enterprise value proposition includes three things. First, the promise of a meaningful customer experience. Second, the capacity to deliver on that promise. And third, the sense of served consequences of both of the above, for stakeholders. For more on this subject, see page 237.

CONSIDER:
[Return on Character, Kiel]
[Leadership Capital Index, Ulrich]
[Market Value Process, Cleland and Bruno]
[The Quest for Value, Stewart]
[The EVA Challenge, Stern and Shiely, Ross]
[The New ROI: Return on Individuals, Bookbinder]
[Unstoppable: Finding Hidden Assets, Zook]

Talent Blocks and Beams

Individual and team competence is a central theme for development, and a major working consideration in this FieldBook. We have explored competence for many years, in different contexts, and the expression of **Talent Blocks and Beams** is the most practical summary we can put in everyday use, in every organizational setting. Here is a brief synopsis:

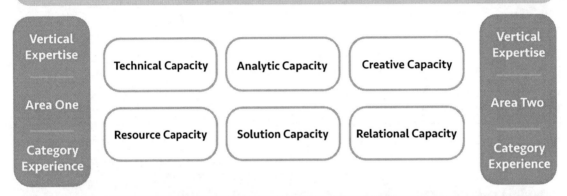

Individual Beam Development

Self-Awareness, Contentment, Character, Self-Governance
Confidence, Moral Compass, Resilience, Motivation, Attention

Vertical Expertise	Technical Capacity	Analytic Capacity	Creative Capacity	Vertical Expertise
Area One	Resource Capacity	Solution Capacity	Relational Capacity	Area Two
Category Experience				Category Experience

Team or Group Beam Development

Social Intelligence, Role Awareness, Maze Sense, Influence
Perspective, Engagement, Conflict Management, Appreciation

Copyright, 2007 - 2019 Dewar Sloan, Daniel Wolf

From this picture of Talent Blocks and Beams, we have the body of **Vertical Expertise** and **Category Experience** that reflect combined knowledge and perspective. We have the collection of **Individual and Collective Development factors** that shape personal, social and cultural attributes. And within these elements, we have six areas of personal and professional acumen that we call **Talent Blocks**. This is the essence of talent, for all intents and purposes. This is the assembly of soft skills and hard skills for Strategic Teams.

CONSIDER:
[Multiple Intelligences, Gardner]
[Men Astutely Trained, McDonough]

Exploring Talent Blocks and Beams Further

The six Talent Blocks are a very important part of the capacity of any organization. Talent is multi-faceted. Talent is born *and* made. Talent is forged in the crucible of experience *and* honed in the work of making strategy happen. Talent is built to serve with purpose.

Organizations have unique and differentiated collections of talent, and these may enable and/or constrain growth, performance and change. The real challenge is to match individual and collective talent to the intentions, projects and challenges of the organization ...

- *Presenting **Technical Capacity** with the need for knowledge, expertise, credentials, translation*

- *Presenting **Analytic Capacity** with the need for information, comprehension, data application*

- *Presenting **Creative Capacity** with the need for innovation, generation, impression, options*

- *Presenting **Resource Capacity** with the need for productivity, leverage, collaboration, standards*

- *Presenting **Solution Capacity** with the need for navigation, correction, advancement, recovery*

- *Presenting **Relational Capacity** with the need for connection, influence, confidence, belonging*

Cultivating the right blend of talent requires more than the normal recruiting, development and retention effort. Organizations with well-curated **talent supply chains** are deeply and seriously engaged in the practice of matching people with strategy and culture.

CONSIDER:
[Purpose-Driven Teams and Leadership, Hyacinth]
[The Meaning Revolution, Kofman]
[Meaning-Making in a Community of Practice, Drath and Palus]
[Man's Search for Meaning, Frankl]
[The Intelligence Puzzle, Williams]
[The Intelligence Trap, Robson]

The Strategic Team and Culture

Effective teams are cultural assets. They express values, principles, standards, habits and norms that make them capable and confident. The general terms of Strategic Teams and culture are summarized below for background purposes. **Culture informs strategy** and **culture guides the platforms that support people making strategy happen.**

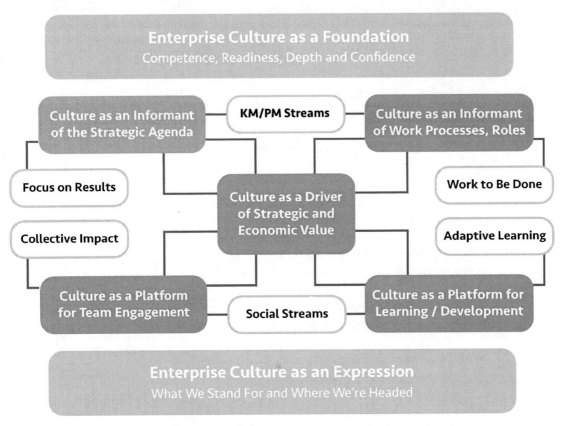

Copyright, 2007 - 2019 Dewar Sloan, Daniel Wolf

Organizational culture is an expression or manifestation of shared vision, norms, principles, values, beliefs, habits, mindset patterns, expectations, attitudes and everyday standards of conduct. Beyond this definition, however, is the importance of organizational culture as a **foundation for and expression of making strategy happen**.

CONSIDER:
[Organizational Culture and Leadership, Schein]
[Unstoppable Teams, Mills]

Culture as a Foundation

When we think of organization culture as a foundation, the main idea builds from the ways in which it informs everyday thought and behavior. Culture is an informant of:

- ***The Strategic Agenda Itself, Focus on Results***
  - *Strategy direction, integration and execution*

- ***The Work Processes and Roles of Strategic Teams***
  - *Work to be done and the roles of individuals*

At this level, with organization culture as a foundation, individuals and teams are gathered and held together by knowledge management and project management streams. These so-called **KM/PM Streams** become the communication and coordination channels that spark, nurture and shape strategic thought and behavior across the organization.

Culture as an Expression

When we turn to organization culture as an expression, the main idea is that people come together, learn, engage, develop and grow, and quite often advance together with essential **social streams.** Culture is a platform that serves:

- ***The Guidance for Team Engagement; Collective Impact***
  - *Common purpose and critical resolve to perform*

- ***The Leverage of Learning and Development; Adaptive Learning***
  - *Access to stakeholder networks, sources of influence*

With organization culture as an expression, individuals and teams are better able to plan forward, make decisions, manage risks, and solve problems. The platform evolves as a part of the organization's DNA, representing the inherent readiness, competence and resolve of the organization to adapt, survive, sustain and prosper. However, the stakeholders of toxic, wayward, meandering, hapless and naive management can be compromised.

CONSIDER:
[Leadership BS: Fixing Workplaces and Careers One Truth at a Time, Pfeffer]
[Principles: Life and Work, Dalio]
[One Team-Discussions that Activate Teamwork, Ross and Paccione]

The Elements of Talent

The six elements that are framed in this FieldBook should be familiar to most of us. They include technical skills and capacity, analytic skills and capacity, creative sense and competence, resource sense and capacity, solution skills and competence, and finally, relational skills and competence. We use the terms capacity, skills, competence and sense broadly in this FieldBook. Individuals and teams harness these elements in different ways, in different forms, and for different tasks. As such, we look at them broadly as learned and developed assets of the organization, elements that engage people as stakeholders in the collective competence of the organization.

What Do Organizations Really Need?

Organizations are communities of people who are tasked with a broad array of work. People are grouped by roles and functions, levels and processes, skills and applications, personal traits and behaviors, capacities and specific competencies. People engage in the goals of the organization in the context of strategy, culture, structure and resources. Some of us are effective role players, and some of us have unique gifts and talents. Some of us are effective leaders and managers, and some of us operate very well in isolation. This is very important because organizations have diverse strategic needs and people come to work with diverse skills, experience, knowledge and styles.

CONSIDER:
[Unlocking Potential, Simpson]
[Agile Team Organization, Hardy]
[Cognitive Diversity and Teams, Pandolfo]
[Diversity and the Talent Economy, Burjek]

Common Needs and Concerns

Organizations *Need* Talent Supply Chains. Talent is generally defined as a balance of specific competence, energy, motivation, connection and persistence. Talented people matched to the organization's Strategic Agenda is a common concern and often a significant challenge. This FieldBook serves as a guide for developing talent supply chains, the streams of talented people with essential knowledge, strength, readiness and depth.

Organizations *Need* Strong Project Teams. Most of the strategic work addressed by organizations depends on project teams that are chartered to tackle challenges and drive progress. Project teams address goals and schedules, tasks and problems, systems and resources, barriers and requirements, processes and value. Project teams:

- *Shape Operational Practice and Excellence*

- *Drive Innovation in Different Forms and Pathways*

- *Frame Systems for Developing, Managing, Advancing*

- *Forge Answers to Questions, Premises, Hassles, Puzzles*

- *Build Pathways for Navigating Strategic Functions*

Organizations have evolved as project management schemes that engage people at different levels in different functions, and as agents who tackle all the key aspects of making strategy happen. Conventional structures and contemporary open structures depend on capable, smart, adaptive, strong project teams. This FieldBook serves as a guide for developing strong project teams, consistent with strong project management discipline and practice.

CONSIDER:
[The Open Organization, Whitehurst]
[The Corporate Lattice, Benko and Anderson]

Organizations *Need* "Strategic Team" Cultures. Organizational culture can be described in terms of everyday thought and behavior that enables individuals and teams to conquer, evolve and advance. Culture is the DNA that connects people making strategy happen and the pulse of people working well together, regardless of social differences and stature. Organizational culture is part character and principle, part exchange and interaction, part passion and perseverance. Individuals and teams express and articulate culture in their everyday thought and behavior. This FieldBook serves as a practical guide for developing Strategic Team cultures and subcultures, with the "gear" to make strategy work.

Organizations *Need* Learning and Development Pathways. Individuals and teams learn how to function and perform in formal and informal ways. Formal teaching and knowledge development extends far beyond the traditional education system for most people today. Learning through experience, discovery, simulation, practice and evolution takes place across the broad array of work we tackle in our roles and assignments. The nature of change puts most individuals and teams under pressure to develop their broader talents. This FieldBook serves as a guide for advanced Learning and Development.

CONSIDER:
[The Speed of Trust, Covey]
[The Innovator's Dilemma, and Disrupting Education, Christensen]
[Learning Investment and Leadership Development, Prokopeak]

Organizations *Need* the Power of Collaboration. Getting strategic work done in concert with other individuals and teams is more and more important across most corporate and nonprofit organizations. We define effective collaboration in terms of people working together to address challenges that cannot be resolved by working separately. Building greater capacity for effective collaboration generally involves:

- *Common Goal Matching*

- *Effective Communication*

- *Responsive Engagement*

- *Dealing with Challenges*

- *Collaboration and Trust*

CONSIDER:
[The Culture of Collaboration, Rosen]

The collective power and impact of organizational collaboration can be impressive. The tensions, conflicts, noise and stresses of collaborative effort can also be impressive. For most organizations, the constraints to collaboration tend to outweigh the incentives for it. This FieldBook serves as a guide for generating effective collaboration.

Organizations *Need* Change Leadership and Management. Few organizations are adequately equipped to drive strategic and operating change, and this area of need reflects the Dual-Dynamic challenges of taking care of today while getting ready for tomorrow. Driving change, coping with change, dealing with change tensions and barriers and guiding change requires attention, engagement, perseverance and adaptation. This FieldBook provides support for integrated change management and leadership.

CONSIDER:
[Breaking the Code of Change, Beer and Nohria]
[The Game-Changer, Lafley and Charan]
[Driving Change, Wind and Main]

Organizations *Need* Team Credibility and Influence. Individuals and teams exchange ideas, perspectives, experiences, knowledge, judgment, assumptions and different frames of view on planning and decision making. They wrestle with information, evidence, political tensions, ambiguity, risk factors and unknowns. They work together to address problems, constraints, opportunity space, options threats and emerging challenges. Personal and professional influence sheds light on the issues, the alternatives, the criteria, and the focus of what is right and wrong, possible and doubtful, certain and dubious. Credibility drives actions and choices. Influence moves people and their everyday behavior. This FieldBook offers support for generating team credibility and effective stakeholder influence.

CONSIDER:
[Becoming a Person of Influence, Maxwell and Dornan]

Organizations *Need* the Everyday Power of Maze Sense. Individuals and teams navigate in the real world of management and problem solving with a sense of attention to, and appreciation of what is really going on in their marketplace and across their organization. Maze Sense is an old phrase that reflects how well we pick up on patterns, signals, values, presence, trust, priorities, power, norms, practices, standards and other factors that shape the conditions in which organizations evolve. Maze Sense is learned and developed through experience and attention, zooming-in and zooming-out on matters that shape opportunities and risks on the marketplace horizon, or in the heart of the organization. This FieldBook provides guidance for the development of Maze Sense for people at every level.

CONSIDER:
[Aristotle's Way, Hall]
[Maze Bright and Maze Dull, Jennings]

Organizations *Need* the Power of Conversation. The "open currency" of team and individual communication is basic human conversation. People connect and interact through conversation. They explore, discover, advance, integrate, prepare, resolve and execute with the advantage of conversation. They engage in constructive, compassionate, fierce and deliberate dialogue about the present, the future and everything in between. They open frontiers with conversation. They correct errors and miscues with conversation. They navigate, expedite, adapt, persevere and survive challenges through conversation. They engage, encourage, support, and correct each other through conversation. They bring together verbal and symbolic cues in conversation. They acquire, arrange and disperse knowledge in conversation. They learn and develop in conversation with and across cultural landings. This FieldBook guides the development of everyday conversation, as a team and individual asset. This is a powerful piece of the equation for Strategic Teams.

CONSIDER:
[Conversational Intelligence, Glaser]

Organizations *Need* the Vision of Smart Aspirations. Individuals and teams operate with a general sense of purpose, vision and mission. Purpose is a big idea, a broad horizon, a great frontier, a grand theme that organizations frame and that individuals and teams serve. People serve with purpose relative to the marketplace and the organization. The point of purpose is, generally speaking, some aspiration, a guidepost, a North Star, a compass of expectations, a better world. A vision of better products and services, better marketplace connections, better technology, better outcomes, collective impact, safer solutions, a better future, greater access, smarter value. The generation of answers to challenges, barriers, constraints and **super-wicked problems.** We depend upon and thrive with smart aspirations. This FieldBook helps shape aspirations that make a difference.

CONSIDER:
[True North, George, Sims and Gergen]
[How We Work, Weiss]

Common Needs and a Path Forward

These ten needs are simple, and they are complex. The organization's response to these needs and concerns is a path forward that is built on a disciplined approach to matching strategy, talent and culture. **That is our intention ... to advance Strategic Teams.**

Foundation for Learning and Development

Organizations are collections of people, systems and practices. Organizations have needs and they often have a platform and a mindset for Learning and Development. The broader view of organization Learning and Development is often connected to purpose, vision and mission, and the so-called Natural Goals for the enterprise. Sometimes, however, Learning and Development is connected only by threads to the organization's Strategic Agenda for growth, performance and change. This FieldBook is designed to broaden the Learning and Development connection with the organization's Strategic Agenda, to embrace needs with:

- *Strong Project Teams*

- *Talent Supply Chains*

- *Strong, Focused Cultures*

- *Learning and Development Pathways*

- *The Power of Collaboration*

- *Change Leadership and Management*

- *The Power of Credibility and Influence*

- *Everyday Power of Maze Sense*

- *The Power of Conversation*

- *Aspirations and Navigation*

Individuals and teams prosper when they weave these ideas together to make a platform that shapes positive everyday thought and behavior, in a manner that effectively drives the organization's Strategic Agenda for growth, performance and change.

People make strategy happen, when they are prepared, engaged and resolved to deliver.

CONSIDER:
[Business is Learning, Prokopeak]
[The Hybrid Skills that Tomorrow's Jobs Will Require, Weber]

Foundation for Leadership and Management

Strategic Teams are organizational assets. They are more or less valuable, and they are the nexus of value creation. Strategic Teams are shaped, for better or for worse, by the leadership and management conditions of the organization. There are at least four levels of leadership and management influencers at work for most people ...

- *Individual, Self-Leadership and Self-Management*
- *Team and Group, Shared and Communal Leadership and Management*
- *Organizational, Leadership and Management Authority, Power*
- *Stakeholders, Beyond the Boundaries of the Organization*

This FieldBook serves as a resource for leadership and management at each of these levels, each with the perspective, knowledge and intentions for making strategy happen.

CONSIDER:
[Super Leadership, Sims and Manz]
[Leadership on the Line, Heifetz and Linsky]
[Leadership 2.0, Bradberry and Greaves]
[Managing Oneself, Drucker]

Foundation for Governance of Organizations

Strategic Teams are part of the governance view of organizations as well. Governing boards are responsible for the oversight of executive leadership and management of the organization's Strategic Agenda. Teams are groupings of human capital.

They are also responsible for operational oversight of growth, performance and change, and the capacity of the organization to deliver on planning, decision making, risk management and problem solving. Strategic Teams, their competence, readiness, resolve and depth are part of the board's assurance of the capacity to perform. They are also a basic indicator of enterprise value, near-term and long-term.

CONSIDER:
[Board Oversight of Talent, NACD Blue Ribbon Report]
[Governance as Leadership, Chait, Ryan and Taylor]
[Corporate Boards, Conger, Lawler, Finegold]

Questions for the Organization

From these foundations, this is a good point to address a few key questions. These are not "one time" questions. They are part of an ongoing conversation, an ongoing exploration of the factors that drive success.

- *How do we define the Strategic Agenda of the organization, and how do different people engage in the everyday work of making the organization's strategy happen?*

- *How do we approach talent in general, and what are the factors that shape the development and cultivation of the organization's talent supply chains?*

- *How do we assess culture as an informant of the Strategic Agenda, and a platform for strategy direction, integration and execution as the organization evolves?*

And another question ... at what point does any of this make a difference in the lives of the organization's stakeholders? Why does this matter to employees, customers, investors, suppliers and partners? How does any of this enhance or constrain value?

What matters in terms of the enterprise value proposition? Does the intended customer experience matter to people at every level? Does the capacity to deliver on that promise engage people in and across functions as agents of making strategy happen? What are the consequences of this stream of efforts to deliver on that experience?

CONSIDER:
[Questions Are the Answer, Gregersen]
[A More Beautiful Question, Berger]
[Anticipate: The Art of Looking Ahead, DeJang]
[A Curious Mind, Grazer and Fishman]
[Humble Inquiry, Schein]
[Zen Mind, Beginner's Mind, Suzuki]
[Ask More: The Power of Questions, Sesno]
[Inevitable Surprises, Schwartz]

CHAPTER 02
THE FRAMEWORK

Talent That Serves with Purpose

Effective organizations depend on individuals and teams who are prepared, connected and resolved to move projects and drive results. That is no small premise. It depends on a framework that **builds talent that serves with purpose and drives Strategic Teams that:**

- *Serve the organization's Strategic Agenda*
  - *Direction, forces and strategic choices*
  - *Integration, alignment of resources, processes*
  - *Execution, actions matched to impact*

- *Serve the organization's culture and values*
  - *Principles, norms, standards, practices*
  - *Personal engagement, leadership and attention*
  - *Everyday thought, character and behavior*

- *Serve the organization's resource model*
  - *Structure and nature of the organization*
  - *Capital, systems and operating capabilities*
  - *Adapting, responding, upgrading, changing*

The teams and performance framework is built on a set of ideas that are part of a capacity and competence model. At the heart of this model is functional talent and character.

Strategic Teams come with the unique capacity to prepare, advance, adapt and sustain in their work and their impact. They have the collective competence to excel in forward planning, decision making, risk management, problem solving and the creation of value. Strategic Teams serve as the engines of progress. They serve with purpose.

CONSIDER:
[Dream Teams, Snow]
[Hardwiring Excellence, Studer]
[Making of a Manager, Zhuo]

Talent Blocks and Beams

Our picture of Talent Blocks and Beams is illustrated below. Other models define mixed Learning and Development streams for individuals along the lines of core knowledge and competence. Talent Blocks and Beams provide a practical approach to individual and team development, building on several dimensions of human capability and human capital.

This framework for Learning and Development speaks to the cultivation, advancement, engagement and sustenance of individual and team capacity across the organization.

Individual Beam Development

Self-Awareness, Contentment, Character, Self-Governance
Confidence, Moral Compass, Resilience, Motivation, Attention

Vertical Expertise	Technical Capacity	Analytic Capacity	Creative Capacity	Vertical Expertise
Area One	Resource Capacity	Solution Capacity	Relational Capacity	Area Two
Category Experience				Category Experience

Team or Group Beam Development

Social Intelligence, Role Awareness, Maze Sense, Influence
Perspective, Engagement, Conflict Management, Appreciation

Copyright 2007 - 2019 Dewar Sloan, Daniel Wolf

CONSIDER:
[Insight, Eurich]
[The Talent Solution, Gubman]
[Leading with Emotional Intelligence, Nadler]
[The Functional Intelligence of Teams, Wolf and Blair]
[Executive Intelligence, Menkes]

Vertical Beams: Expertise and Experience

Most of us have a working base of know-how, expertise, skillsets, competence and attention. This may reflect specific training and credentials, or perhaps a body of work experience and exposure. This **primary base** is our main vertical beam. Some of us have significant exposure to a **secondary base** of knowledge or expertise as well, flanking our main areas of expertise and experience. Building depth and scope of experience in more than one area is a good idea.

> Think about:
>
> - *Engineers with solid financial system knowledge*
>
> - *Machine operators with strong science know-how*
>
> - *Accountants with savvy design process skills, sense*
>
> - *Nurse practitioners with strong informatics skills*

Some of us have backgrounds in general studies, liberal arts, performing arts, the ministry, the school of hard knocks, social services and other fields. This kind of knowledge serves as a broader, differential base for vertical depth and scope. A broader differential base has certain advantages that reveal themselves over time, in different settings and circumstances.

Horizontal Beams: Personal and Social Development

The horizontal aspects of our experience and attention connect our individual and team competence. The **individual beam** reflects our self-awareness, contentment, character and self-governance assets. These help us deal with our moral compass, our confidence, passions, motivation, drive, happiness, resilience and the ownership of what really matters to us as human beings. Who are we, and why do we engage in things the way we do? What makes us tick, and why? What makes us behave the way we do, as agents of grace or perhaps, complete jerkwagons who undermine or counter the goodness in other people?

The **team or group beam** reflects how and why we function as members of a community, a project team, a congregation, communal group or interest group. This team or group beam portrays our social intelligence, role awareness, cultural savvy, political sense and capacity for influence. These help us deal with other people in a common journey, the challenges of working with stakeholders, with or without conflict, or a clear charter for doing whatever we are supposed to do with each other. Who are we, and why do we engage with others the way we do? What makes us capable of contributing to team progress? What matters most?

Talent Blocks and Background

Our ability to perform as individuals and team members is a mash-up of six elements. These define our Talent Blocks, the guts of this Learning and Development framework.

Technical Capacity	Analytic Capacity	Creative Capacity	Resource Capacity	Solution Capacity	Relational Capacity

These Talent Blocks reflect a wide range of influences and experiences, from the dynamics of neurobiology to the lessons of life revealed. Exposure and experience clearly matter a great deal. Individual DNA and temperament play a significant role. Gender differences, expressed in biological and cultural patterns are also part of the development equation. Socioeconomic, generational and sociocultural factors temper our everyday thought and behavior within and across these six Talent Blocks.

Situational experience is an important and powerful ingredient in the formation and sustenance of these blocks ...

Think about:

- *How youthful mischief and/or protection relates to creativity, relationships, problem solving, risk behavior*

- *How strict attention, order and task compliance serve to shape technical, analytic and resource thinking*

Much of this book is devoted to the balance of strategic team awareness and behavior, the development of collective competence, and the everyday work of making strategy happen. Talent Blocks and Beams are raw material for **Strategic Teams and Development**.

CONSIDER:
[The Talent Code, Coyle]
[Dark Horse, Ogas and Rose]
[Talent Management, Goldsmith and Carter]

Talent Blocks and the Roadmap

- **Technical Capacity and Competence** reflects the product of our knowledge base, subject matter expertise, operating know-how and/or technical credentials. Technical capacity and competence is covered in **Chapter 03** of this FieldBook.

- **Analytic Capacity and Competence** incorporates our sense of data, systems, patterns, signals, measures, markers and their cause-and-effect connections. Analytic capacity and competence is covered in **Chapter 04** of this FieldBook.

- **Creative Capacity and Competence** reflects our ability to come up with new ideas, new points of view, new ways of sensing, thinking, doing and serving. Creative capacity and competence is covered in **Chapter 05** of this FieldBook.

- **Resource Capacity and Competence** is about appropriation and how we use human capital, systems, time, money, and a range of hard and soft assets to get things done. Resource capacity and competence is covered in **Chapter 06** of this FieldBook.

- **Solution Capacity and Competence** is the product of problem recognition, signal sense and diagnostic practice, problem navigation and resolution. Solution capacity and competence is covered in **Chapter 07** of this FieldBook.

- **Relational Capacity and Competence** is about connecting with others, engaging and getting along, bringing out the best in others, growing together. Relational capacity and competence is covered in **Chapter 08** of this FieldBook.

These elements are clearly not all that mysterious. Philosophers and sages have pondered these elements since dirt was new. Educators have tested them in Learning and Development practice for generations. Individuals choose vocations, causes, soul mates, experiences, friends, passions, interests and employers with their influence. Organizations review, select, promote, engage, develop and discharge people on the basis of these elements. These Talent Blocks enable and/or constrain success at different levels.

Our personal and communal sense of who we are, what we stand for, how we gauge ourselves, and our connections with others depend on these six elements. Our combined competence, character and connections emerge in the sum of these elements of our everyday thought and behavior. **We become an expression of these elements in action.**

Talent and Strategy Engagement

The term engagement means many things. In broad terms, engagement means the degree to which people are committed to a cause. To be highly engaged, we need to understand and approach the cause, our role in advancing the cause, and our connection with others who have roles in advancing the cause. We need to understand the prospective impact and consequences of our efforts relative to the cause, and our communal respect for others who are more or less engaged in the cause of the organization. Engagement is a big deal.

Patterns of Strategy Engagement

The research, and common observations, tell us that most organizations have people engagement scores that vary from dismal to terrific. Depending on specific diagnostics, common strategy engagement patterns tend to show up as follows:

- **Lower Engagement.** In these organizations, the combined engagement levels reflect weak attention to the Strategic Agenda, relatively low regard for the development of people, and a weak and/or stratified culture.

- **Modest Engagement.** These organizations exhibit some level of interest in objectives and priorities, and general regard for talent and collaboration. However, the engagement of these organizations tend to be mixed.

- **Better Engagement**. These organizations show deliberate efforts to connect people, strategy and value, they work to match talent, functions, relationships and leadership roles. They have positive, but often understated cultures.

- **Great Engagement.** These organizations have gained from commitments to Learning and Development, the exchange of strategic ideas and values, the enhancement of resources, the advancement of culture and good governance.

CONSIDER:
[Above the Line, Henderson]
[Agile Engagement: Lasting Results, Jaramillo and Richardson]
[Fierce Loyalty, Mallam]
[Big Potential, Achor]
[How to Win Friends and Influence People, Carnegie]
[Employee Engagement 2.0, Kruse]
[Three Culture Conversations: CEO/HR, Working Paper on Tech/Culture, Gartner]

Challenges

Standing in the way of many organizations are naturally generated barriers and constraints. These arise and propagate in most organizations, at one level or another. They reflect the technical, market and economic forces of the environment. They reflect in the cognitive, functional, emotional and behavioral streams of the organization itself. These challenges translate in the terms of:

- The Nature and Demands of the New/Next Customer

- The Relative Advantages of Core/Disruptive Competitors

- The Compliance Requirements of the Business Category

- The Economic Tensions and Pressures on the Enterprise

- The Alignment of Operations, Channels and Supply Chains

- The Organization's Options to Business Model Evolution

- The Attraction, Engagement and Sustenance of People

- The Relative Interests of Employees as Stakeholders

Strategic Teams and Development connects these issues with a framework that is geared to readiness and resolve. Strategic Teams, in their more advanced state of development, are the principal source of competitive advantage, enterprise evolution, performance and corporate sustenance. Over time, and as conditions change.

CONSIDER:
[Humility is the New Smart, Hess and Ludwig]
[Principle-Centered Leadership, Covey]
[The Significance Principle, Carter and Underwood]
[The Rise and Fall of Strategic Planning, Mintzberg]
[Digital Transformation, Siebel]
[KAOSPILOT A-Z, Elbaek and Associates]

Engagement: What Matters?

The stronger the engagement, the stronger the prospects for success as organizations navigate their Strategic Agenda. Engagement levels, specific to the organization's Strategic Agenda, vary widely in reflection of four basic factors:

- *How well individuals and teams understand the general direction, integration and execution aspects of the Strategic Agenda.*

- *How relevant these aspects of the strategic agenda are viewed by individuals and teams, relative to their general and specific roles in the organization and their interfaces with other stakeholders, internal and external.*

- *How well connected individuals and teams sense they are with the organization's purpose and the nuances of the Strategic Agenda.*

- *How much passion, energy, perseverance, trust and power that individuals are willing to crank-up for the cause, for the journey, for the work of making the Strategic Agenda happen.*

In those organizations where strategy engagement is greater, individuals and teams may see themselves as **agents of the Strategic Agenda**. That simple idea, that basic mindset of people as agents of the Strategic Agenda, is clearly a huge deal for any organization.

CONSIDER:
[The Alliance, Casnocha, Yeh and Hoffman]
[Prepared and Resolved: The Strategic Agenda for Growth, Performance and Change, Wolf]

Strategy Engagement: The Elements

The most important markers of strategy engagement can also be viewed in terms that reflect a set of criteria that we offer as check points for FieldBook users. Consider the following themes in strategy engagement. These are common descriptive and behavioral themes that tie strategy engagement together. There is some overlap, but each stands on its own as part of the everyday thought and behavior that drives individuals and teams ...

Intentional Learning and Discovery. *Engagement means that people balance the interests of the organization with the volatility, uncertainty, complexity and ambiguity, or the "VUCA," of their strategy environment. Working through complex and dynamic issues in business demands a certain level of exploration, risk taking, adaptation, attitude change, endurance and solid expeditionary habits. People who travel the discovery paths of business life do so because it seems necessary, and because they need adventure.*

Commitment and Accountability. *Engagement means that people assume a level of technical, social, emotional and economic responsibility for activity and results. It strongly suggests interdependence and membership. It blends leadership assets and management discipline to model commitment and accountability. Some people come to this theme because they are responsive to measures and targets. Others are motivated by the charge to attack the most difficult stretch challenges of the business.*

Personal Talent and Enthusiasm. *Engagement means that people bring their capabilities, passions, perspectives and motivation to the Strategic Agenda, and they influence the development of "leadership assets" across the organization. Leadership assets are the collective assets of individuals and groups who make things happen. Enthusiasm is one part energy, one part passion, and one part ethics of performance. And the talent equation for most organizations is that which blends together capability, motivation and connections.*

Interpersonal Effort and Influence. *Engagement means influence and advocacy as well as the recognition and integration of differences in perspectives, backgrounds, resources, capabilities and subcultures. The influence factor in strategy engagement is catalytic. Influence reflects on the system of interactions and the culture and subcultures of the organization. It spans the enterprise, touching on anxieties, risks, desires, goals and the company's sense of what is possible and worthwhile. Effort is framed in a "Lean Context" for our purposes here.*

Systems, Order, and Arrangement. *Engagement means the orderly and systematic treatment of everyday decision making, problem solving and forward planning. Structures, routines, and processes serve this need for arrangement. Processes and project management schemes provide both content and context for behavior and interaction, and for the most part, these frameworks guide thoughtful decision making and problem solving. They encourage productivity, and under the right circumstance, they can encourage strategic thinking.*

Discretionary Effort and Innovation. *Engagement means the inspiration to stretch out toward challenging targets and ventures. It also means the persistence to continue on difficult tasks and experimental work until they yield results. Discretionary effort is personal and collective. The greater impact of discretionary effort is the model it provides for people as they work across spaces in strategy integration and execution. The very hard work of business innovation is almost always powered by discretionary effort and resolve.*

Effective, Systemic Collaboration. *Engagement means working together across the boundaries of the organization. Communication practices, partnership behaviors and goal alignment are key variables in effective collaboration. Organizations are systems and they operate in evolutionary ways to match business capability and opportunity. There are common incentives, as well as constraints, to effective collaboration. These reflect structure, culture, resources and strategy, and also determine the creation and capture of value.*

Appreciation and Human Respect. *Engagement means thoughtful devotion to the cause, empathetic response to challenges and shared values, business goals, confidence, purpose and trust in one another that guide and nourish effort. Strategy engagement is a human endeavor. It involves conflict, emotions, power, challenges, persona, tensions, rewards and thoughtful devotion to the cause. Leadership and management of the Strategic Agenda requires people to rise above themselves into a more prospective, conductive and supportive role.*

Each of these themes of engagement is important as a stand-alone idea, but in combination, they present a powerful organizational construct. When people absorb and embrace these ideas, stakeholders are more prepared and resolved to get things done. In the context of the Strategic Agenda, across the board, that means more attention and energy devoted to the organization's strategy direction, integration and execution work.

Team Culture of Impact

Individuals and teams may function at high levels, scoring results, outcomes, progress and impact. The potential for high-functioning teams is naturally higher than low-functioning teams that lack focus, a sense of purpose, and the drive for impact.

This **culture of impact** is learned and developed at the individual and team level, over time and through experience. It reflects many of the strategy engagement themes outlined in the previous pages. It demonstrates a positive mindset for growth, performance and change. This culture of impact is part of **what it means to serve with purpose,** adapt and respond, learn and advance. It speaks to our ability to deal with uncertainty and ambiguity, conflict and tension. It frames the everyday thought and behavior that individuals and teams express in their work and in their lives. This connects ambition and purpose, insight and horizon-mapping.

This culture of impact is essential DNA for individuals and teams, creating value, making strategy happen. Impact may be a matter of opportunity, luck, challenge and environment. However, and more likely, impact is a function of preparation, determination, coordination and serious cultural concentration on what matters and how to get things done in the routine, and under pressure.

CONSIDER:
[Approaches to Cultural Assessment, Cameron and Quinn]
[The Culture Code, Coyle]
[Good to Great, Collins]
[Great By Choice, Collins and Hansen]
[The New Corporate Cultures, Deal and Kennedy]
[An Everyone Culture, Kegan and Lahey]

Team Culture of Excellence

Organizations compete on the basis of product and service advantage, operating systems and resources, market and customer connections, development capabilities, reputation assets and value stream advantage. Cranking-up any of these factors provides at least some power to win, to succeed, to make progress, advance and prosper. When organizations get cranked-up on these fronts, the culture of excellence becomes real and robust. The culture of excellence breeds value.

This culture of excellence is another "epigenetic" marker of solid individual and team capacity and competence. It builds on the collective efforts and achievements of people who clearly view themselves and their colleagues as agents of the organization's Strategic Agenda.

CONSIDER:
[The Excellence Dividend, Peters]
[Operational Excellence, Issar and Navon]

Culture is an expression of the way things are done, what people believe, the habits of the organization. Culture is also an ongoing informant of strategy, and of key resources that drive success. Culture is also a valuable platform for team engagement and for team Learning and Development.

Culture is tied to strategy, resources, structure and cadence on the pace at which things are attended to, brought together, driven to results. And with most organizations, the team **culture of excellence is really a mosaic of subcultures**, with smaller dispersed groups and functions that make things happen in and across the organization.

The Promise of Teams

Most of what organizations achieve today is the result of very capable individuals working together in some kind of team or group construct. The nature of people working together, of collaborating, of teaming-up in partnerships, of self-directing and integrating and progress making, these are part of the great promises and the great horizons of teams.

The structure and assumed powers of teams also deserves attention. Different kinds of teams, team order and arrangement, team authority and influence, shape team focus. Team constraints and boundaries, team incentives, team functions, roles, risks, roadmaps, policies, practices and processes. These are all part of the team leadership and management equation for the organization, and these factors make or break teams.

CONSIDER:
[No More Teams!, Scharge]
[Team of Teams, McChrystal]
[The Critical Few, Katzenbach, Thomas and Anderson]
[The Wisdom of Teams, Katzenbach and Smith]

And, Why We May Struggle With Teams

The counter to the promise of teams is important to understand. The "trouble" with Strategic Teams and their efforts are manifested in everything from weak leadership and management to weak match-ups of talent. The "trouble" with Strategic Teams also stem from the curation of strategy, culture and structure, and the hard and soft governance of what matters, why it matters, how it matters and for whom it matters.

CONSIDER:
[Start with Why, Sinek]
[The Five Dysfunctions of a Team, Lencioni]
[Team of Rivals, Goodwin]
[The Six Mistakes of Man, Cicero]
[The Power of a Positive Team, Gordon]

Types of Teams

When we think of the promise of teams, many images and examples flood our perspectives. The contents of this FieldBook have been applied in a wide range of settings, including:

- **Executive Teams**
  - *Senior leadership and management roles, priorities*

- **Project Teams**
  - *Formally and otherwise chartered and commissioned*

- **Program Teams**
  - *Designated to develop, integrate, execute programs*

- **Process Improvement Teams**
  - *Designed to drive better, smarter, faster ... more value*

- **Advance Teams**
  - *Designed to prepare the ground ahead, ready-making*

- **Tiger/Surge Teams**
  - *Assigned to accelerate priorities with focus and force*

- **Functional Teams**
  - *Representing an organizational zone of practice roles*

- **Expeditionary Teams**
  - *Designed to explore, navigate, confront and discover*

- **Recovery Teams**
  - *Designated to follow-up, review, remediate, resolve*

- **Governance Teams**
  - *Assigned from board leadership and committee roles*

And the list goes on ...Red Teams, Insight Teams, Gray Teams. Many types of teams, in many settings, with many roles and different levels of power, energy and trust. They all matter ... Implementation Teams, Discovery Teams, Turnaround Teams and more. 20 types of teams.

The Evolution of Teams

Where do we gather our sense of teams and teamwork? Where do we, as individuals, learn about teams and teamwork? What about changing roles in different kinds of teams? Where do we begin to appreciate the good, the bad and the ugly of teams and teamwork? For most of us, the answers to these questions begin to stream together in our younger years: in school, with our friends, in sports, music, play, early work, group functions, clubs. They form in the streets, the arts, camps, and a host of curricular and extracurricular activities that range from robotics camp to theater camp to hacker camp to orchestra/band camp to writer camp, sports camp and elsewhere.

As we move into adulthood, we gain deeper team perspectives and exposure from ongoing education, work assignments, task force activity, military service, community service, parenting, professional collaboration, teaching, coaching, guiding, managing, leading, helping and **serving with purpose**. Experience and perspective …

Most of us have a pretty good sense of what makes for good team players by early adulthood. At about the same time, we pull together a sense of what we do not like about teams and teamwork, and individual behaviors that can also pollute and corrode our view of **teams and teamwork**.

CONSIDER:
[Team Human, Rushkoff]
[The Upside of Conflict, Fowler, Field and McMahon]
[Business Architecture, Ulrich and McWhorter]

Personal Roles on Teams

We also have different roles for ourselves as individuals, as members of teams, in the work of teams, with teams in conflict and teams in success. Most of us will have the opportunity to serve different team roles, with different responsibilities and evolving power and trust. Depending on our individual character traits, we may serve teams as **compliance** masters, **integration** masters or **exploration** masters. We may have influence or authority over each and perhaps all of these roles in different settings and circumstances.

Think about:

Compliance - *Focused on rules of order and standards of work*

Integration - *Focused on bringing working elements together*

Exploration - *Focused on the new/next thing, the future horizon*

CONSIDER:
[Character, Strategy and Leadership: The Seneca Project, Wolf]
[The Importance of Experience and the Impact on Leadership, Gallup]
[Personality and Temperament in Teams, Gerke and Berens]
[Turning Team Performance Inside Out, Nash]

Some of us are natural leaders and/or managers, and yes indeed, there is a difference between leadership and management. **Effective leadership of teams** and teamwork pivots on perspective, aspiration, confidence and perseverance. **Managing teams and teamwork** pivots on information, procedures, measurement and navigation. **One part leadership,** matched well with **one part management,** and both are key anchors for effective and adaptive teams and teamwork. It becomes essential that we develop both. For further review of the range of roles and tasks on work teams, see page 236 on *Team Assessment*.

CONSIDER:
[Self-Leadership, Self-Management, Self-Governance, Wolf]
[The Social Animal, Brooks]

Ongoing Team Development

| Purpose | Guidance | Practice | Change |

The presence or absence of these development themes explains most of the differences between teams that get things done and those that muddle. This is true for both talent-rich teams and teams short on core talent. Some teams make up for their "short bench" with good hard work, deep trust, smart moves, group cohesion, true courage, maze sense and a kind of "bloody-minded" perseverance that just powers its way through the badlands.

Think about:

- **How to convey and sustain purpose**
  - *What is purpose-driven?*

- **How to provide positive guidance**
  - *What is positive mindset?*

- **How to arrange for future-readiness**
  - *Preparation, practice, more practice*

- **How to gather buy-in for change**
  - *From urgency to action*

The Dual-Dynamic nature of an organization's Strategic Agenda is the biggest reason for ongoing team development. The near-term will evolve as part of the long-term. The knack required for early development will evolve as the organization matures. The Talent Blocks that are blended for one program will differ from those required for another. Nothing stays the same, change is ongoing, evolution is reality. Strategic Teams serve in this Dual-Dynamic realm, under conditions that are never fixed, as **agents of making strategy happen.**

CONSIDER:
[Leadership the Army Way: Be, Know, Do, Hesselbein and Shinseki]
[Buy In, Kotter and Whitehead; A Sense of Urgency, Kotter]
[The Dichotomy of Leadership, Willink and Babin]

Development and Transformation: Discipline

Several factors shape the conversation on team development. First, and really most important is the purpose of teams. We develop individual talent and collective talent to address some **purpose**, and that can be tied to the organization's broader Strategic Agenda or to a specific project, function or task. **A team without a purpose is an empty set.** People matched to purpose is always the starting point, the focus, the sense-maker for individual team development. People serving with purpose is a key engagement marker.

Second, in order to advance individuals and teams, we need some **guidance** in the form of leadership and management, some order and focus, arrangement, integration and quite often, some course correction. Guidance can come from policy governance, formal learning and development processes, coaching, and the right kind of intervention, navigation, support and personal counsel. Effective guidance moves team development forward with trust.

Next, team development depends on **practice** and steady engagement. Teams emerge, develop and evolve in their capacity and competence based on deliberate practice and commitment to programs, then commitment to excellence, then commitment to mastery. At some point, team development comes face-to-face with transformative options and challenges. When that time comes, teams take on a performance leadership role.

Fourth, individual talent, team structures and the work of teams **change** at different rates and levels. People come into team structures as newbies, and as veterans, as cultural envoys and as refugees from other teams and organizations, whether good, bad or ugly. New team synthesis and engagement is a curious journey, with many influences, attitudes, concerns and incentives – all melded together. Teams evolve constantly, they morph, they reform and they disperse. Teams change, and teams are powerful agents of change.

When teams come together, as they work together, as they advance together and as they grow together, these four Learning and Development guideposts are critical.

CONSIDER:
[Development Notes for Prepared and Resolved, Wolf and Swartzendruber]
[Great Organizations, Collins, Porras and Hansen]
[A Passion for Excellence, Peters and Austin]
[Humans are Underrated, Machines and Humans, Colvin]

Teams and Transformation

At the intersection of the organization's Strategic Agenda for growth, performance and change are talented people with capacity and competence. Most people in organizations work together with others in some kind of team or group system. They bring their respective hard and soft skills to the game. They bring their attitudes, beliefs, habits, influence, trust, and authority to the work of making strategy happen. They learn from experience, from the lessons of progress, from the culture of teams. They grow in self-knowledge and confidence along the way. They learn from tension, from mistakes, from failure.

As the technical, operating, market and economic winds of change blow across the marketplace and the organization, team development takes on a powerful and challenging role across the work of transformation.

Change emerges in simple policy and process form, broader program and operating form, and sometimes, in business model form. Teams are the integrators and executors of change. They deal with the roadmap for change, the barriers to change and the navigation of change itself. Teams enable or constrain the buy-in of others. Teams persuade and encourage people to take part in routine change initiatives, and transformation.

Surely, character and confidence are part of the broader transformative work of teams and individuals. Big change is demanding and consuming and rich with tension. Big, transformative change often leaves components of the organization behind, structurally and culturally. This alters everything for organizations, teams and individuals.

CONSIDER:
[Transformational Leadership, Riggio and Bass]
[The Leadership Roadmap, Baumgardner and Scaffede]
[Launching a Leadership Revolution, Brady and Woodward]

Advancing Responsibility

As we consider our personal and professional view of Talent Blocks and Beams, our individual and team development issues, our specific areas of capacity and competence, a couple of things should be part of our exploration. First, what do we, as individuals bring to the table? Second, how do we work well with others? In the following pages of this FieldBook, the answers should become clear, for individuals and for teams.

Think about:

- **Where are you with regard to:**
    - *Individual Beam Development?*
    - *Self-Awareness, Character, Self-Governance?*
    - *Confidence, Motivation, Attention, Constructs?*
    - *Career Status, Vertical Expertise, Experience?*

- **Where are you with regard to:**
    - *Talent Blocks and Area Strengths?*
    - *Talent Blocks and Challenges, Gaps, Concerns?*
    - *Talent Blocks and Leading with Others on Teams?*
    - *Talent Blocks, and the Work to Be Done?*

Teams and Talent: Bottom Line

The bottom line of Talent Blocks and Beams can be expressed in terms of greater engagement, with lower barriers to resources, more productivity, discovery and compliance, better collective impact, greater contentment and more effective efforts on growth, performance and change.

Teams are effectively engaged, or not, as agents of the Strategic Agenda.

Effective teams drive the creation of both strategic and economic value.

PART 2
INDIVIDUAL AND TEAM CAPACITY

The strength of the team is the individual member.
The strength of each member is the team.

Phil Jackson

Find a group of people who challenge and inspire you,
spend a lot of time with them, and it will change your life.

Amy Poehler

We fight as a single, impenetrable unit.
That is the source of our strength.

King Leonidas

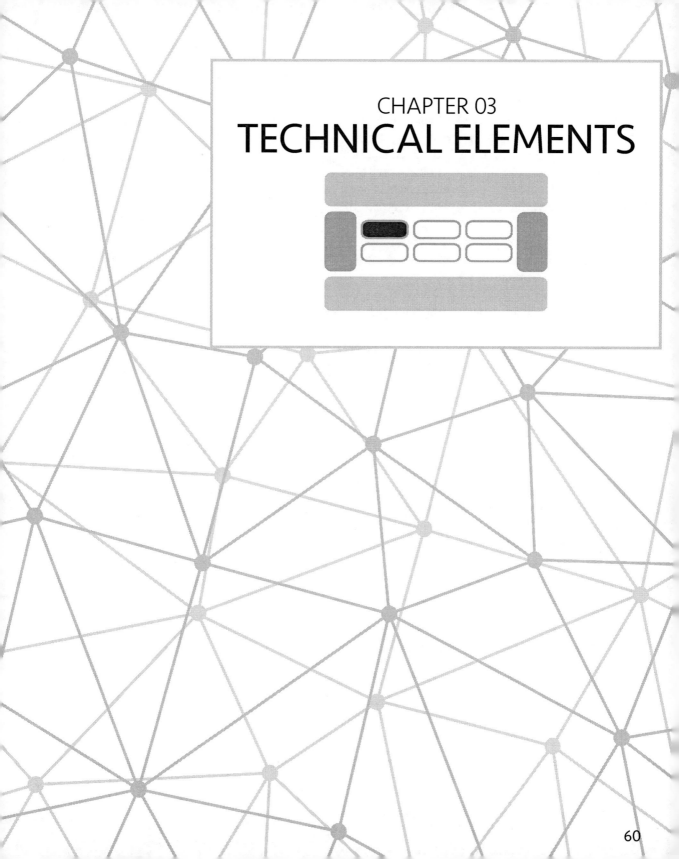

CHAPTER 03
TECHNICAL ELEMENTS

Introduction

Technical capacity and competence are reflected in subject matter knowledge in a specific field. We develop levels of expertise in specific areas and that enables us to address our roles with skills, abilities and knack. People with strong technical savvy may also bring higher levels of confidence to their work, as individuals, and within their respective teams.

We can see technical capacity and competence in a wide range of roles and applications, and those may include everything from scientific work to artistic performance, design engineering to media management, financial analysis to social psychology. Everywhere we see the need to organize, arrange and apply particular knowledge to our work or our other roles in the world, we are dealing with technical capacity and competence.

Technical knowledge and content are learned from study and experience. While some people may have natural interests and abilities in an area or function, the capacity to organize and apply technical knowledge depends on learning experiences and exposure. The exposure we have as young people clearly influences the knowledge we absorb as we develop in our roles over the journey of life. Environment matters.

CONSIDER:
[Range: Generalists, Epstein]
[The Wisdom of Experts, King]
[The Expertise Economy, Palmer and Blake]
[Technical Leadership, Carullo]
[Applied Minds: How Engineers Think, Madhavan]

Key Areas - Technical

For individuals, teams and organizations, the nature of technical capacity and competence can be examined in operational terms in five key areas.

- ***Knowledge Management, or KM***
  - *The acquisition, arrangement and application of knowledge*

- ***Subject Matter Expertise, or Deep KM***
  - *The connections, frameworks and integration of knowledge*

- ***Learning Models and Structures***
  - *The approaches, pathways and architecture of knowledge*

- ***Adaptive Know-How and Practice***
  - *The dynamic organization and application of knowledge*

- ***Theory Making and Data Sense***
  - *The acumen to generate and cultivate new knowledge platforms*

These are the key points of technical capacity and competence, reflected in how we acquire, arrange and apply knowledge. These provide the subject matter expertise that organizations need to function. These provide the substance for working together on content and on challenges. These enable individuals and teams to function effectively and with confidence as they engage in their various roles and obligations.

Further Detail - Technical

We can examine each of these areas further, and in doing so, we can pose some questions that should help to bring the elements into perspective. These questions help define the everyday nature and usage of technical capacity and competence.

Knowledge Management, or KM

What is the so-called Body of Knowledge that is most relevant to our work? Which sources of knowledge are important, and which are most relevant or valuable? How do we know the aspects of knowledge that are essential and those which may be supplemental or adjacent? These and other questions about knowledge management are part of our quest for technical capacity and competence.

Subject Matter Expertise, or Deep KM

What are the building blocks of technical capacity and how do we assemble and connect the components of knowledge that are the foundation of expertise? How do areas of knowledge relate to one another, and are they subject to tension? How does new knowledge map together with existing knowledge? What are the authority powers of knowledge and expertise, and who determines what knowledge is the correct and proper knowledge? What knowledge conflicts exist?

CONSIDER:
[The Power of KM, Hunter]
[Deep Smarts, Leonard and Swap]
[KM World, Knowledge Management Journal]

Learning Models and Structures

Where and how do we acquire knowledge? What are the natural channels of Learning and Development for a specific type of knowledge, or a broader body of knowledge? How do we best gather new knowledge and balance our inventory of knowledge? How do we access knowledge? How do we learn to organize and arrange knowledge in ways that are practical and convenient? How do we test and challenge knowledge, in theory and in practice? What is the structure?

Adaptive Know-How and Practice

Where do we apply the knowledge and expertise we have, and how do we match what we know with situations and challenges? What makes us capable of tapping knowledge and expertise from different areas to address problems, opportunities and conflicts? What is the power of knowledge when we confront volatile and ambiguous threats, or new challenges or uncharted barriers? How do we bend and shape our know-how to deal with tough conditions and difficult people? How do we adapt to new technical norms?

CONSIDER:
[The Knowledge Link, Badaracco]
[Educating Intuition, Hogarth]
[Peak: The New Science of Expertise, Ericsson and Pool]
[Wellsprings of Knowledge, Leonard-Barton]
[Introducing the Knowledge Athlete, Taghavi]
[The Wealth of Knowledge, Stewart]

Theory Making and Data Sense

Much of what we call knowledge and expertise starts with a blend of theory and data. What is the guiding theory of the field of practice, and who made it known? How does the current body of knowledge apply in everyday thought and practice? Where does new data that supports or advances or refutes existing theory come from? Who are the theory makers and what is their relevance in the field of subject matter and practice? How do we test and challenge theory? What is the governing body, or sector power of knowledge for the team, the organization?

Knowledge management has evolved as a major technical discipline with broad roots in Learning and Development, information management, research and evaluation, communication systems and collective human curiosity. Knowledge is evolutionary and dynamic. Knowledge management is a practice that enhances technical capacity and competence in ways that advance the interests of individuals, groups and organizations. So we ask ourselves, what difference does any of this make in our roles? What difference does it make in the charge of teams? Who says?

CONSIDER:
[The Fifth Discipline, Senge]
[Knowledge Engineering, Adeli]
[What a Successful AI Team Looks Like, Korolov]
[Human + Machine, Daugherty and Wilson]
[Artificial Intelligence in Practice, Marr and Ward]

Development Considerations

Technical capacity and competence is something we build through learning and experience. What we build and how we build it are shaped by needs and conditions. Developing the technical capacity of individuals and groups and entire organizations depends on practical engagement across four areas:

- **Leadership and Management View**
  - *What matters, and why is technical competence important?*

- **Common Indicators and Criteria**
  - *What are the practical markers of technical competence?*

- **Experiential Learning Approach and Focus**
  - *What is the roadmap for technical capacity and competence?*

- **Connecting with the Other Elements**
  - *What makes technical competence relevant to our roles?*

Most of us work in roles that have some connection to the technical foundations of an institution, an organization or a social cause. Some of us are responsible for the core technical capacity and competence of the enterprise. Some of us are operatives, working in the application and exchange of that technical capacity with stakeholders in the organization, and beyond. Some of us serve in administrative or functional roles not directly tied to technical capacity and competence. Our direct engagement may vary, but we are all dependent on technical capacity and competence. We also interact with others who depend on basic technical insights.

Leadership and Management View

Who determines what counts in technical competence and who guides the general process acquisition, arrangement and application of technical capacity across the organization? What is the process of subject matter development and management? What about the perspectives and aspirations of individuals and groups shapes the leadership of technical capacity? Who governs what happens to standard content and theory in practice over time, and on what points do we change? Where is the contemplation?

Common Indicators and Criteria

What is the meaning of basic, table stakes awareness in the arena of technical capacity? What is mastery level and maturity in technical competence? How do we learn the elements of technical capacity and how is our progress measured, gauged, recognized and rewarded? Which indicators of accomplishment are clear and which are subject to some ambiguity and tension? What is the relevance of credentials? And are there different credentialing powers?

CONSIDER:
[Five Dimensions of Quality, Suskie]

Experiential Learning Approach and Focus

Some technical sense may be innate, but much of our technical smarts and savvy is learned through experience. What kind of experience drives technical capacity and competence? What does experience teach us about technical expertise? Where do we find technical knowledge, and how do we organize and arrange technical knowledge assets? How do we use technical knowledge in practice? Can we program specific experiences that forge technical capacity? Experience counts. Who gauges experience value?

Connecting with the Other Elements

Technical capacity is naturally part of our individual and group expression of capability. Our technical capacity goes with our creative, analytic, resource, solution and relational abilities to shape our total capability set. Some of us with high technical capacity and maturity work very well with others, and some don't. How do leaders bring forth their appreciation for and interfaces with technical matters that are important to the team? How do we connect individual KM assets across the organization? And, how do we anticipate the new/next in technical and technological subjects? Who plays in the connector space?

CONSIDER:
[Professional Learning Communities, Dufor]
[Leading in a Culture of Change, Fullan]
[Borrowing Brilliance, Murray]

Check Points - Technical

As we look over the challenges and objectives that define our roles, there are several check points that are worthy of consideration. These help us gather a set of lenses for understanding technical capacity, what matters, how things connect and apply and how they contribute to the collective impact of people making strategy happen.

Intentional Questions ...
Purpose, Roles, Challenges, Risks

What is the scope and range of technical capacity and competence required of the role, the organization, the sector? What could or should technical capacity mean for stakeholders? How does technical capacity figure in the evolution of the organization?

Standard Diagnostics ...
Thoughts on Assessment and Evaluation

There are many ways to test for technical capacity and for the purposes of this FieldBook, we are agnostic about specific measures or assessments. However, we are advocates for the use of differential analysis and diagnostic models that frame technical skills and sense.

Developmental Guidelines ...
Learning/Development

Technical capacity does not fall out of the clouds, although a range of themes may serve our technical interests. Every individual and group deserves a set of specific guidelines that help shape the expectations and evolutionary assets for Learning and Development in the area of technical capacity, and in collateral areas of strategic teamwork.

Engaging ...
Standard, Powerful, Effective and Savvy

More engaged individuals, groups and organizations take the case for technical capacity learning exposure to higher levels of effort. The so-called culture of perpetual Learning and Development is something that goes very well with technical capacity as knowledge itself is dynamic. Engagement depends on conversations that connect people and ideas.

More Detail, in Context

Breaking things down even further, we can entertain additional themes and details in the area of technical capacity and competence with more probes and points for discussion.

Intentional Questions ...
Purpose, Roles, Challenges, Risks

We could begin the assessment of technical capacity and competence in the context of need and purpose. Why is technical capacity relevant? Why are we concerned about the subject matter and content that shape the organization's focus, purpose, goals and horizons? Why does any particular aspect of technical capacity matter to stakeholders? What about this area of teamwork really matters? What difference does any of this make for teams?

Standard Diagnostics ...
Thoughts on Assessment and Evaluation

While many technical fields are gauged by credentials, degrees, measures of expertise, subject matter classifications and other markers, what really counts depends on the setting and conditions. Some fields require 20 page CVs and badges that cover the jacket. What matters? Other fields require more broadly defined measures of technical competence, often pointing to specific achievements as opposed to credentials. How do we gauge the value of background and exposure? Which assessment tools are best for the review of technical capacity? Sometimes, technical competence is hard to gauge and tough to distinguish.

Developmental Guidelines ...
Learning and Development

Much of what we understand and practice was learned at some point, in academic terms and/or through everyday experience. Some Learning and Development pathways are clearly expressed and well posted. Others are more difficult to discern and navigate. What, given the nature of the subject matter itself, are the major pathways, knowledge base and theory branches of the field? Across every setting, what do we need to attend to in the construction and maintenance of the right Learning and Development platforms?

Engaging ...
Standard, Powerful, Effective and Savvy

When teams are highly engaged in technical matters, our people are probably thoughtful, motivated and connected in the subject matter. Technical attention tends to shape technical interest, and technical interest tends to move technical learning, activity and results. How do we drive attention? When we have lower engagement, our people may express their general concern about technical matters, but they are less likely to do much about the technical priorities and resources of the organization. How do we keep people on task and on track?

How does the everyday thought and behavior of the broader **organization** reflect on the development and integration of technical competence? How do we, **as individuals**, look at technical capacity and competence as a murky and mysterious function, or as a matter of intentional leadership and management. How do these interact? How do they put us in conflict? How do we support and sustain technical capacity and competence in teams?

CONSIDER:
[The Competitive Imperative of Learning, Edmondson]

Summary – Technical Elements

Focused technical capacity, knowledge, expertise and competence is part of the story for every individual, group, team and organization. In the broadest terms, technical matters define what an organization provides and how it operates. Technical capacity frames what an individual and group or organization could do, or should do, or in some cases, must do. It establishes the ground on which competing interests are favored or passed over, leveraged or wasted. It is substantive.

Technical does not mean scientific or mathematical to the exclusion of the aesthetic and philosophical. Technical capacity relates to theory and practice, concepts and applications, widgets and stacks, forms, methods and outputs. This is the greater bounty and value we can discover, exchange, express and advance with technical capacity.

Think about:

- *The key areas of technical capacity*

- *How these contribute to team capacity*

- *How these complement other Talent Blocks*

- *The targets of team/technical development*

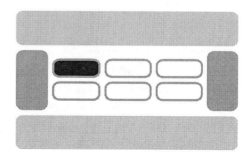

Summary Audit: Technical Capacity

Introduction

Organizations have diverse needs and requirements for Technical Capacity, and they also have different approaches to Learning and Development. The intent of this summary audit of Technical Capacity is simply to connect some themes for gauging the relevance, applications and measures that go with Technical Capacity. This audit approach can be modified to match the interests and requirements of the organization with talent development pathways that make the most sense for individuals and teams.

Technical Capacity and Competence

- ### *Knowledge Management, or KM*

  General Considerations ...
  - *situations, challenges*

  Development Considerations ...
  - *alternatives, horizons*

- ### *Subject Matter Expertise, Deep KM*

  General Considerations ...
  - *situations, challenges*

  Development Considerations ...
  - *alternatives, horizons*

- ***Learning Models and Structures***

  General Considerations ...
  - *situations, challenges*

  Development Considerations ...
  - *alternatives, horizons*

- ***Adaptive Know-How and Practice***

  General Considerations ...
  - *situations, challenges*

  Development Considerations ...
  - *alternatives, horizons*

- ***Theory Making and Data Sense***

  General Considerations ...
  - *situations, challenges*

  Development Considerations ...
  - *alternatives, horizons*

Collective Impact and Implications

Near-Term and Long-Term Themes

Notebook

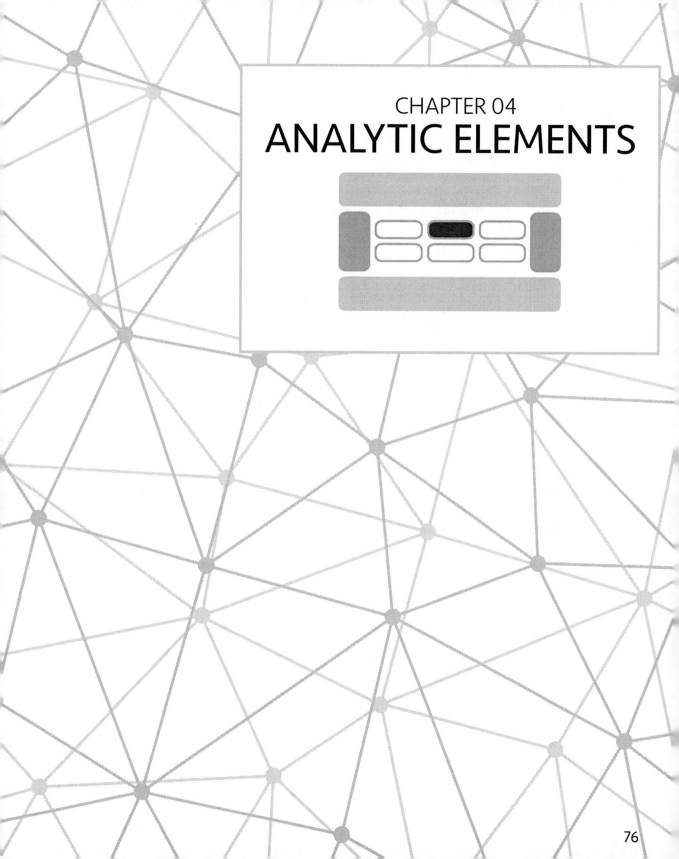

CHAPTER 04
ANALYTIC ELEMENTS

Introduction

Analytic capacity and competence are reflected in perspectives and methods that shape our clear understanding of **facts and truth**. We develop a level of reasoning about situations and objects that enables us to better understand cause and effect, comparative value and positive and negative confirmation. People with strong analytic savvy may also bring high levels of insight and judgment for decision making, problem solving and risk management.

We can see analytic capacity and competence in a wide span of roles and responsibilities, and those may include everything from advanced decision science work to the everyday work of execution in the field, on the line, and in the realm of systematic, repetitive work. Everywhere we see the need to sort through root causes, social noise, disruptive forces, common patterns, bodies of work and emerging issues, we are dealing at some level with analytic capacity and competence. This is how we rise above bias.

Analytic capacity and competence are learned from study and experience, and while some people are naturally geared to logic models and systems thinking, the broader capacity to apply basic analytic skills and processes is generally built through formal Learning and Development. The exposure we have in the cause of our expanding experiences is the stuff that hones our knack in the realm of analytic capacity and competence. Analytic agility is part of the mix.

CONSIDER:
[Weaponized LIES, Levitin]
[Thinking, Fast and Slow, Kahneman]
[Systems Thinking, Gharajedaghi]
[Industrial Dynamics, Forrester]
[Critical Systems Thinking, Jackson]

Key Areas - Analytic

For individuals, teams and organizations as a whole, analytic capacity and competence can be examined in practical terms under the headings below.

- **Contextual Understanding**
  - *Environmental sense and operating views that provide greater insight*

- **System Assessment**
  - *Situation awareness and landscape lenses that reflect whole environments*

- **Attention to Causality and Origins**
  - *View of dependent and independent variables that connect and collide, show cause*

- **Comparison and Contrast**
  - *Sense of differences and similarities that make each factor more relevant*

- **Logic and Perspective**
  - *Sense of argument, influence, judgment and narrative that shed light*

These are the key points of analytic capacity and competence. These reflect how we approach information, points of view, data sets, the absence of data, historical facts, prospective trends, patterns of movement and association, conflicts, narratives and the paradoxes that surround decision making and risk management. Analytic skills and practices enable individuals, groups and organizations to function effectively, and with confidence in their roles.

Further Detail - Analytic

We can examine each of these areas further, and in the process, we can pose questions and themes that should provide further insight into practice. These questions should help define the everyday issues of analytic activity and analytic processes.

Contextual Understanding

What is the context of a challenge, problem or a conflict that we need to better understand? What are the political and/or cultural forces that inform the operating views of the organization? What about leadership insight and management depth? What about the smoke and haze that often surround the decision making or risk management process? What does the structural and compliance picture look like? Context shapes our perspectives, grounding and perceptions of and about key forces and trends.

System Assessment

When we look at a new situation, how readily do we see the moving parts, the primary forces, the dimensions and constructs, the boundaries and barriers, the challenges and concerns? What are the key indicators, the triggers, the points of tension, the incentives and values? What are the resources of power and change? What are the nodes and links? These and other questions about analytic work and condition assessment are the starting points for planning and decision making.

CONSIDER:
[System Analysis and Design, Satzinger]

Attention to Causality and Origins

From the start, what are the preconditions and causes that may shape a situation or a process or a practice? What do we really know about the cause and effect relationships that shape a situation? What causes problems or challenges? What are the origins of trouble, of opportunity and motives? Where did the culture of exploration or integration or accountability emerge from? Why should we care about cause and effect, now and for the future? What about changes in focus? What about future causes and effects?

Comparison and Contrast

How we find patterns, how we gauge differences, why we believe in things, why we respond to things and how we view right and wrong are aspects of comparison and contrast. What things are alike, and why bother with them? What things are different, and again why should we care? How do some things appear similar, when in fact, they are not at all alike? Why do we hold biases in our choices and preferences? Why indeed. How do we manage to entertain ideas that may, at times, be founded by opposing logic models?

CONSIDER:
[Factfulness, Rosling]
[Critical Thinking, Chatfield]
[Damned Lies and Statistics, Best]
[Analytics at Work, Davenport, Harris and Morison]
[The Upside: The 7 Strategies, Slywotzky]

Logic and Perspective

Some of us are consistently drawn to logical choices and preferences, logical sequences, logical decisions and actions. Some of us have a preference for the path less traveled, the alternative to the norm, the contrary choice. What lies behind these perspectives, behaviors and preferences? What powers shape our individual and group logic models? What biases get in the way of rational choices with optional value? This, in many ways, is the source of many a human dilemma.

Human history is rich with analytic contributions in the sciences, the arts and culture, medicine, design, education and navigation. Analytic capacity has been part of warfare, politics, literature, design, science, agriculture and romantic quarrels since the dawn of civilization. Advances in information science and data aggregation have shaped a new dawn of business analytics, and Artificial Intelligence has opened the gates for discovery, integration and compliance speed. So we again ask ourselves, what difference does any of this really make for teams in action?

CONSIDER:
[The Infinite Game, Sinek]
[The Decision Model, von Halle and Goldberg]
[The Model Thinker, Page]
[Creating Great Choices, Riel and Martin]
[Quirky: Breakthrough Innovators, Schilling]
[Models for Critical Thinking, Rutherford]

Development Considerations

As with the other elements, analytic capacity and competence is something we learn and develop, through formal and informal experience. What we develop is shaped by the general analytic tasks we entertain in our functions and roles. How we develop more powerful analytic skills depends on practice and engagement in four areas:

- ***Leadership and Management View***
  - *What matters, and why is analytic competence important?*

- ***Common Indicators and Criteria***
  - *What are the practical markers of analytic competence?*

- ***Experiential Learning Approach and Focus***
  - *What is the roadmap for analytic capacity and competence?*

- ***Connecting with the Other Elements***
  - *What makes analytic competence relevant to our roles?*

Most of us work in roles that have some connection to analytic processes and outputs. Some of us are responsible for concentrated analytic work and the convergence and integration of that work in decision making, forward planning, risk management and problem solving. Some of us are essentially users of analytic processes, data and throughput. Some of us participate on the front-end of analytic work, others on the back-end. Some of us gather the resources and processes for analytic work while others work as recipients and agents for data analytic outputs.

Leadership and Management View

How we lead and manage analytic capability is drawing more attention in every sector, due in part to Big Data options, and to systems that support better decision making and risk management processes. Who sets the tone for analytics? What analytic tools and resources are needed? How do teams sort through and apply the insights and throughput of analytic work? What kind of communication processes are best for the collection, management and dispersion of analytic work? What kind of governance is practical for guiding analytic capacity and competence?

Common Indicators and Criteria

What does strong analytic capacity and performance mean for organizations and their stakeholders? What are the essential markers of analytic maturity and mastery, and what kind of guideposts should we use to gauge the development of analytic capacity and competence? How do we scope out the right kind of Learning and Development tracks for analytic capability? With regard to that, how do we score progress and how do we recognize performance in everyday analytic work and broader analytic engagement? What are the practical measures of superior analytic capability? And what about specific credentials in analytics? What about the new and next frontiers of cognitive automation?

Experiential Learning Approach and Focus

Analytic skills are acquired through different kinds of Learning and Development streams. Basic skills and knowledge sets are important table stakes for analytic work. General literacy, mental agility, general acumen, math ability, system sense and other assets are good foundations. However, the practical weapons of analytic capacity and competence are forged and based in experience. What about our development of logic and reasoning skills? Where do we generate differential diagnostic skills? How do we gain our ability to understand and predict outcomes and prescribe pathways? Experience matters, and the art and science of Analytics moves on with simulation, data power, Artificial Intelligence and synthetic methods applied to enterprise processes.

Connecting with the Other Elements

Analytic capacity relates to each of the other five elements of individual and group capability … technical, creative, resource, solution and relational skills. Some of us whose acquired and natural gifts include analytic mastery are especially valuable on teams that have significant challenges to address, changes to navigate and practices that must be fine-tuned. How do we match individuals with strong analytic senses and capacities as helpful catalysts on teams that are charged with priority setting and resource matching? How do we engage analytic practices in a cultural frame?

Check Points - Analytic

Each member of a team contributes their talent to the cause, and those individuals with analytic strengths are duty-bound to bring out the analytic sense of others. Analytic work in teams enables the generation of insights that support **zooming-in and zooming-out**.

Intentional Questions ...
Purpose, Roles, Challenges, Risks

What is the scope and range of analytic capacity and competence that is required in key roles in the organization? What could or should analytic capacity mean in different functions of the organization, across functions, with teams and prospects? How does analytic capacity figure in the evolution of the enterprise?

Standard Diagnostics ...
Thoughts on Assessment and Evaluation

Specific tests for analytic skills are outside the scope of this FieldBook, but organizations are wise to explore the best ways to set the analytic Learning and Development map for individuals and teams. General logic models and math skills, statistical know-how, decision science and computational sense are foundations, along with communication skills.

Developmental Guidelines ...
Learning and Development Protocol

Analytic capacity is built through experience, on foundations mentioned above. Experience with observations, experiments, situation and response models, project simulation, data management and model construction are among the popular vehicles for Learning and Development. More simulation in Learning and Development is a natural horizon.

Engaging ...
Standard, Powerful, Effective and Savvy

Building analytic talent with individuals and groups, and across the organization requires true engagement and cultural support. When expectations are high for analytic rigor, speed, reach, depth and power, people will generally grow and respond to the needs and temperament of the organization. However, no tension often means no engagement, because the team may not be stretched to respond to challenges and options.

More Detail, in Context

Taking the analytic Learning and Development agenda a few steps further, we can examine the nuances and details in this area with some additional probes.

Intentional Questions ...
Purpose, Roles, Challenges, Risks

Analytic capacity and competence brings the perspective and the context needed to choose options, manage risks, and deploy plans and people in order to drive results. The idea of **analytics-on-purpose** is simple ... we need to guide actions and choices. Why is analytic capacity relevant at every level of a team? What can we say about analytic thought and behavior as a piece of the cultural equation of the organization? Who on the team, or across the enterprise is best equipped to marshall the analytic Learning and Development process?

Standard Diagnostics ...
Thoughts on Assessment and Evaluation

Higher education is one of the main arenas for analytic skill development and evaluation. Until recently, specific degree programs provided the grounding for analytic work in the sciences, technology, business, engineering and general studies. Increasingly, business schools, design schools and liberal arts programs are featuring analytic studies. What about less formal pathways? What about diagnostic and assessment markers? How can teams merge their analytic focus, more or less quantitative, more or less qualitative, and more or less supported by effective analytic communication?

CONSIDER:
[Predictive Analytics, Siegel]
[Competing on Analytics, Davenport and Harris]
[Business Unintelligence - Beyond Analytics, Devlin]
[Data Analytics Made Accessible, Maheshwari]

Developmental Guidelines ...
Learning and Development Protocol

How we approach problems and opportunities is important. Talent that is defined along the lines of analytic capacity and competence is shaped through development plans that may be very ordered, or quite informal. We can look at three levels of analytic Learning and Development. First, there are basic analytic tools and precepts that are used and applied broadly. What are these? Second, there are advanced qualitative and quantitative methods, and again these apply broadly. How are these applied? And third, there are task-specific and track-specific methods that are tied to specific roles and tasks. These points suggest the need for a more formal and ordered approach to analytic Learning and Development.

Engaging ...
Standard, Powerful, Effective and Savvy

When a project team or a functional group is highly engaged in analytic work, what is the spark? Attention levels and acumen tend to burn a little hotter. Curiosity, intensity, constructive skepticism, open debate, civil discourse, consideration, contemplative review, speed of trust and other behaviors tend to accelerate in higher engagement, high analytic settings. How do leaders at every level crank-up the analytics? Where credibility of decisions and experiments and arguments are at stake, the **analytic "culture card"** is valuable. Who guides analytic culture and subculture? Who governs analytic priorities and resources?

How does everyday thought and behavior gain from analytic capacity and competence? How do we encourage and support analytic skills at every level of the organization? How do we intervene when analytic weaknesses impact planning options, decision making, risk management and problem solving? At some point, somebody has to take responsibility.

Summary – Analytic Elements

Analytic capacity emerges with experience, and from formal education. The way we view the world, our sense of patterns and influence, our integration with data sets and relationships and our view of cause and effect all shape our ability to ask the right questions and shape the best answers. Analytic capacity defines how we approach challenges, objectives and constraints, and it frames how we create and capture value in a dynamic and ambiguous environment.

Analytic does not mean data-grinding, atom-cracking work. Although for some teams, the atom-cracking and data-grinding aspects of analytic work are part of the joy and the hunt for truth. Analytic savvy does not mean one's confinement to a particular model or method or mindset. Analytic capacity and competence become the fire-starter for exploration and evaluation.

Think about:

- *The key areas of analytic capacity*

- *How these contribute to team capacity*

- *How these complement other Talent Blocks*

- *The targets of team/analytic development*

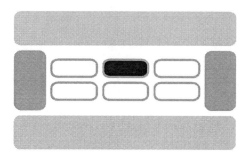

Summary Audit: Analytic Capacity

Introduction

Organizations have diverse needs and requirements for Analytic Capacity, and they also have different approaches to Learning and Development. The intent of this summary audit of Analytic Capacity is simply to connect some themes for gauging the relevance, applications and measures that go with Analytic Capacity. This audit approach can be modified to match the interests and requirements of the organization with talent development pathways that make the most sense for individuals and teams.

Analytic Capacity and Competence

- ***Contextual Understanding***

  General Considerations ...
  - *situations, challenges*

  Development Considerations ...
  - *alternatives, horizons*

- ***System Assessment***

  General Considerations ...
  - *situations, challenges*

  Development Considerations ...
  - *alternatives, horizons*

- ***Attention to Causality and Origins***

  General Considerations ...
  - *situations, challenges*

  Development Considerations ...
  - *alternatives, horizons*

- **Comparison and Contrast**

  General Considerations ...
  - *situations, challenges*

  Development Considerations ...
  - *alternatives, horizons*

- ***Logic and Perspective***

  General Considerations ...
  - *situations, challenges*

  Development Considerations ...
  - *alternatives, horizons*

Collective Impact and Implications

Near-Term and Long-Term Themes

Notebook

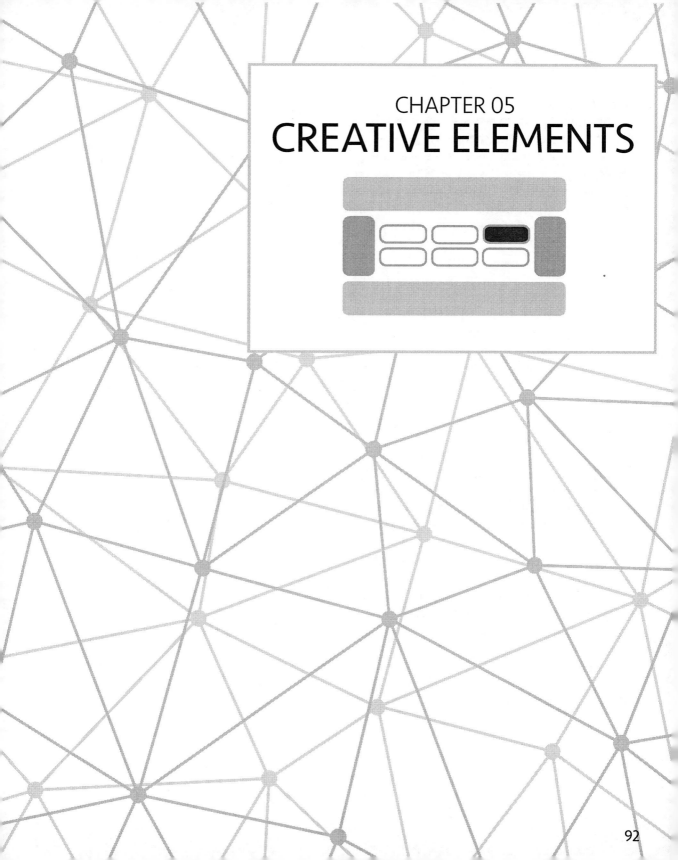

CHAPTER 05
CREATIVE ELEMENTS

Introduction

Creative capacity and competence powers how organizations approach new ideas, address their challenges and deal with change. We generate new frames of experience and new levels of strategic and economic value through the creative work of individuals and groups. Creative skills provide essential bridges between the norms of today and the needs of tomorrow. These skills can drive transformation.

We can see creative energy and talent at work in a wide range of settings, from the development of new products and services to the resolution of complex challenges, to the encouragement of critical conversations. We can tap creative people to tackle new frontiers with combinations of old and new ideas, old and new methods, old and new models. We can build on established work in new collaborative settings and structures. We can solve conflicts, build bridges.

Creative thought and practice can be learned and developed from a combination of study and experience. Creative work is sometimes solitary work, and sometimes accomplished in group mode. Serendipitous insights and interactions can spawn creative flashes and moments of creative insight. The tensions of events and situations can also spark creative thought and remarkably creative behavior. We cultivate the capacity to create in different settings, with different people, with different resources and structures. We can remove barriers and doubt.

CONSIDER:
[Creativity: Flow and Discovery, Csikszentmihalyi]
[A Whack on the Side of the Head, Von Oech]
[Where Good Ideas Come From, Johnson]
[How to Get Ideas, Foster]

Key Areas - Creative

From a broad range of settings, we can isolate five powerful areas of creative capacity and competence that are likely to develop in organizations.

- **Determined Practice**
  - *Discretionary focus on creative experience and creative interaction with others*

- **Leadership Sensitivity**
  - *Awareness, empathy, receptiveness, context-savvy, open to influence*

- **Subject Matter Fluency**
  - *Attention to elements, media, connections, tensions, content alternatives, options*

- **Constructive Imagination**
  - *Intrigue, curiosity with blank space, white space, expeditionary work, horizons*

- **Confidence in Action**
  - *Security of self; comfort with creative flow, confidence in confidence alone*

These are key points of creative capacity and competence, reflected in how we come to view ideas, pivot points, road blocks, norms, values and new paths. These points serve as context and energy for creative work, and they have the potential to inform and influence the creative work of other individuals and groups. Some people may stumble into creative options, and others may take a highly organized path in search of options that are better, easier or faster.

CONSIDER:
[Switch: How to Change Things, Heath and Heath]

Further Detail - Creative

We can examine each of these points in more detail, with questions that both deepen and broaden the applications of creative capacity and competence. In each area, we have framed questions and probes for team and group discussion.

Determined Practice

What kind of working focus supports the ignition and growth of new ideas and alternatives? What do writers, engineers, physicians, soldiers and artists bring to the creative table? What is so important about persistence and passion in creative work? What role does regular creative practice play in building creative capability and competence? What happens when we skip practice? What happens in pre-practice?

Leadership Sensitivity

Awareness is a big, big deal in creativity. Awareness of the interests and needs of people, with awareness defined in stakeholder terms. How do we build a level of leadership sensitivity that promotes and encourages creativity? How do we help secure the work world for creative types? What does empathy do for creative types? What if more people had more protection from threats to the creative process and from outcome risks? What kind of setting is best for shaping creative throughput? What are the water-hazards of creative work? What renews creative passion?

CONSIDER:
[Creativity Inc., Catmull]
[Creative Construction, Pisano]

Subject Matter Fluency

Individuals and groups who think about the connections between farm animals and architecture are likely to have an open mindset and their own version of imaging lenses or virtual reality. What helps people navigate through subjects in different media? What makes them more likely to connect and view some things that lead them to other new things? What drives subject matter fluency as creative currency for individuals and groups? How does **improvisation** power subject matter fluency, in different forms? How do ideas connect across the spans of subject matter?

Constructive Imagination

Curiosity is fuel. What are we curious about, and why are we curious about some things in the context of others? Some individuals and groups come to the creative zone with broad humor, with seemingly odd reference points and even some mild hallucinations. What triggers the imagination? Who is able to hold disparate thoughts and images close? Why does the imagination wander when we're exposed to physical and other sensory touch points and touch streams? What can team members do to engage their collective body of imagination? What fuels the journey?

CONSIDER:
[Creative Confidence, Kelley and Kelley]
[Why: What Makes Us Curious?, Livio]
[Making Ideas Happen, Belsky]
[Lateral Thinking: Creativity Step by Step, de Bono]

Confidence in Action

What does confidence do for individuals who set out to create things in the white space or the blank space of a category? How is confidence developed, cultivated and dispersed in project work that depends on high creative power? What degrades or destroys creative confidence, and what can be done about creative blockage and constraint? What kind of activity or event is helpful in the restoration of creative capacity and competence? How is confidence rebuilt?

Most people have some creative DNA in their realm of service and work. Creative capacity and competence evolve from needs and from practice, and often, these blend and bond together. Song writers get creative by writing. Coders get creative from coding. Designers get creative by conceiving ideas and translating them to some kind of active scheme, with physical and conceptual prototypes. How do we power-up the creative performance of any organization?

CONSIDER:
[Loonshots: Crazy Ideas that Transform, Bahcall]
[How to Kill Creativity, Amabile]
[Strategy Needs Creativity, Brandenburger]

Development Considerations

Creative capacity and competence is partly innate and broadly subject to Learning and Development streams. How we create new stuff reflects our neurological makeup and the launch pads that we occupy in our work with our adaptive mindsets. Making creative work more productive and valuable depends on several factors.

Creative capacity is something we learn in formal and informal ways, in disciplined practice and everyday experience. What we are able to build is shaped by our experience, our roles and backgrounds, the way we engage ideas with others, and the way we govern ourselves. Consider:

- **Leadership and Management View**
  - *What matters, and why is creative competence important?*

- **Common Indicators and Criteria**
  - *What are the practical markers of creative competence?*

- **Experiential Learning Approach and Focus**
  - *What is the roadmap for creative capacity and competence?*

- **Connecting with the Other Elements**
  - *What makes creative competence relevant to our roles?*

Most of us have creative bones, and that's a great thing because our world needs all the creative power we can muster. We need creative options for social welfare, commercial interests, public good and national security. We need creativity for knocking down disease, raising up the generations and dealing with oppression.

Leadership and Management View

How we manage and lead creative capability is more relevant across the span of organizations than most of us realize. The sources of creative spark range broadly. How do we bring these sparks out more readily and how do we set the right conditions for people to think deeply and work with curiosity, grit and humor? How do we set ourselves in motion to use the creative assets we have and to use our own creative knack to engage the creative knack of others? What kind of leadership and management effort guides, motivates, cultivates, curates and rewards everyday creative thought and behavior? What can we do as individuals and teams to make creative practice and general creativity part of everything we pursue?

Common Indicators and Criteria

What does the power of creative capacity look like, sound like and feel like in our world, in our roles? What kind of descriptors do we use to reflect on someone's creative inputs and efforts? What sort of process or scheme contributes to creative throughput? What are the conditions that advance and/or constrain creativity? How do we scope out the right approach for different creative efforts and objectives? How do we match the personas and temperaments of people who work together to come up with creative options and innovation? What is the task at hand and how do we gauge the nature of creative capacity against creative intention? What does a creative team do well for the balance of the enterprise? What about blind spots?

Experiential Learning Approach and Focus

Creative skills are gathered in Learning and Development streams that may have been formed in art class, the woods, in dreams, at the movies, in games, under the stars, and in just about any formal or informal experience where we had to sense the nature of ideas. Most of us get creative in practice, when we need to be creative. We learn to address situations and challenges with ideas. We battle one set of ideas with other sets of ideas. We learn to exchange ideas and argue about ideas and enhance ideas. What do we gain from creativity? What gets in the way of our creativity? What do we need in order to exploit the creative capacity we have? What do we risk by passing over the creativity of others?

Connecting with the Other Elements

Creative capacity and competence relates to the other elements in our framework of thought and behavior. Creative skills come through in the lattice of technical, analytic, resource, solution and relational skills. How do these gain traction together? Some of us are just particularly creative in nature and interaction; how can we serve as powerful catalysts for project teams and groups? For some, creative work is solitary work. For others, the improvised dance of creativity is a group effort, a social process, a cultural endeavor of great collective impact. How do the solo actors inform and influence the broader work of the team?

Check Points - Creative

Teams have an advantage in the collective skills and energy of the people involved. Creative types can ignite team behavior, and the benefits are often felt by individuals who grow in the culture and subculture of creativity.

Intentional Questions ...
Purpose, Roles, Challenges, Risks

What is the scope and range of creative capacity and competence that is useful in key roles in the organization? What could or should creative skills mean in different functions and work processes? What kind of projects demand the power of creative capacity and competence? Are there times when creative types should be silent? What does it take to bring them out of their silence?

Standard Diagnostics ...
Thoughts on Assessment and Evaluation

Assessments can define creative propensities and the cognitive assets that go with creative capacity and competence. However, creative depth and discipline are reflective of so many things in one's knowledge, habit and experience. Creative indicators may reflect in lateral and metaphorical thinking, open-minded view points and simple curiosity.

Developmental Guidelines ...
Learning/Development

We contend that creative capacity is built through experience and patterns of practice. The kind of experience that powers creative skills is broad and diverse, from exposure to the classics to mischief. Clever goes with creative, and sometimes the really clever ones are those with plenty of experience getting out of trouble or avoiding it.

Engaging ...
Standard, Powerful, Effective and Savvy

Building creative talent with individuals and groups, and further, across the organization, requires practice and iteration. Trial and error, more trial and error, and a culture of dealing with creative throughput that is subject to judgment are part of the habit-building nature of creative skill development. There are social and cultural risks to absorb in creative work. Individuals and teams need persistence to sustain them through the creative journey.

More Detail, in Context

Moving further on the creative Learning and Development track, we can take the exploration further with additional questions and reflections.

Intentional Questions ...
Purpose, Roles, Challenges, Risks

Creative capacity provides new looks and new lenses to the science of planning and innovation, thinking through challenges, and mapping out the options and implications for decision making. We need creative juice to advance ideas and draw forth new ways of thinking about stakeholder needs and interests, and the many risks in play. What brings out the creative power and perspective in teams? How do creative types stimulate strategic conversations? How do creative debates escalate? How do creative debates stall out and wither away? What does creative leadership look like? How do organizations attract creative talent? How do they put creative passion and process at risk?

Standard Diagnostics ...
Thoughts on Assessment and Evaluation

Getting a measure on creative capacity at the individual or group level is tough without looking directly in the eye of experience. Can we measure creative assets? Probably, to some extent, we can get a marker or two on curiosity traits, discovery sense, pattern perspective and paradox sense. We might also look for sense of humor, verbal acuity, improv sense and speed of thought as behavioral assets that often tie to creative capacity and competence. What makes diversity a factor in creativity? What about behaviors that block or inhibit creative capacity? What about the emotional considerations of creativity?

CONSIDER:
[Cognitive Surplus, Shirky]
[The Runaway Species, Brandt and Eagleman]

Developmental Guidelines ...
Learning/Development

Some of us become our most creative when we immerse in subject matter in quiet or remote settings. Reflection matters, and anything we can do to shape reflection tends to enable creative thought and behavior. Others need more noise and tension, more stimulation, more interaction to the point of provoking others into creative exchanges. How do we learn these creative tracks, and how might we match teams with similar or different creative appetites? What kind of structured and unstructured Learning and Development would make the most sense for people in the trenches, and their managers? What about contemplation?

Engaging ...
Standard, Powerful, Effective and Savvy

When creative capacity is central to an organization's purpose and culture, there are communication and process norms that carry through in everyday language. How are interactions tempered by the creative views and biases of individuals and project teams? How do some teams build their own creative code? Why do some groups gather the catalytic power to impact team members and stakeholders? In what ways do managers "get wise" to appreciate the creative temperature of groups, along with what it takes to get them cranking and sparking with creative effort and throughput?

How do organizations succeed and prosper on the bounty of creative capacity and competence? What are the natural challenges of plugging creative efforts into different aspects of strategy integration and execution? What about dealing with difficult people who seem to disrupt and diminish creative thought and behavior? Other than by title and rank, who really leads the creative competence of the organization? Always good to double-check that answer. And who advocates for the creative practices of the enterprise?

CONSIDER:
[The Curiosity Gene, Kourt]
[The Velocity Advantage, Bergstrand]
[Powers of Two, Shenk]
[Originals, Grant]

Summary – Creative Elements

Creative capacity powers growth, performance and change. It is cultural and objective, random and systemic, patterned and disruptive. Creativity burns hot in some instances, and it provides an eternal flame in those settings where creative assets are central to an organization's purpose and value streams. Creative assets are a source of competitive advantage and a source of energy. Sometimes that is joyous and sometimes it seeds the grand nasty tensions.

CONSIDER:
[Leonardo da Vinci, Isaacson]

Creative does not mean silly-season, or "scattered playground" excursions with extra doses of stimulation. But it might. Creative does not mean one percent inspiration and the rest perspiration. But it might. Consistently strong creative capacity across the organization is like other intangible assets in that the evidence will not be reflected on the balance sheet, but rather in organic development speed and a propensity for new and different. Creative capacity is not always messy, or restless or anxious. However ...

Think about:

- *The key areas of creative capacity*

- *How these contribute to team capacity*

- *How these complement other Talent Blocks*

- *The targets of team/creative development*

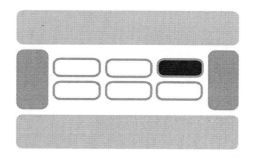

Summary Audit: Creative Capacity

Introduction

Organizations have diverse needs and requirements for Creative Capacity, and they also have different approaches to Learning and Development. The intent of this summary audit of Creative Capacity is simply to connect some themes for gauging the relevance, applications and measures that go with Creative Capacity. This audit approach can be modified to match the interests and requirements of the organization with talent development pathways that make the most sense for individuals and teams.

Creative Capacity and Competence

- ***Determined Practice***

  General Considerations ...
  - *situations, challenges*

  Development Considerations ...
  - *alternatives, horizons*

- ***Leadership Sensitivity***

  General Considerations ...
  - *situations, challenges*

  Development Considerations ...
  - *alternatives, horizons*

- ***Subject Matter Fluency***

  General Considerations ...
      - situations, challenges

  Development Considerations ...
      - alternatives, horizons

- **Constructive Imagination**

  General Considerations ...
      - situations, challenges

  Development Considerations ...
      - alternatives, horizons

- **Confidence in Action**

  General Considerations ...
      - situations, challenges

  Development Considerations ...
      - alternatives, horizons

Collective Impact and Implications

Near-Term and Long-Term Themes

Notebook

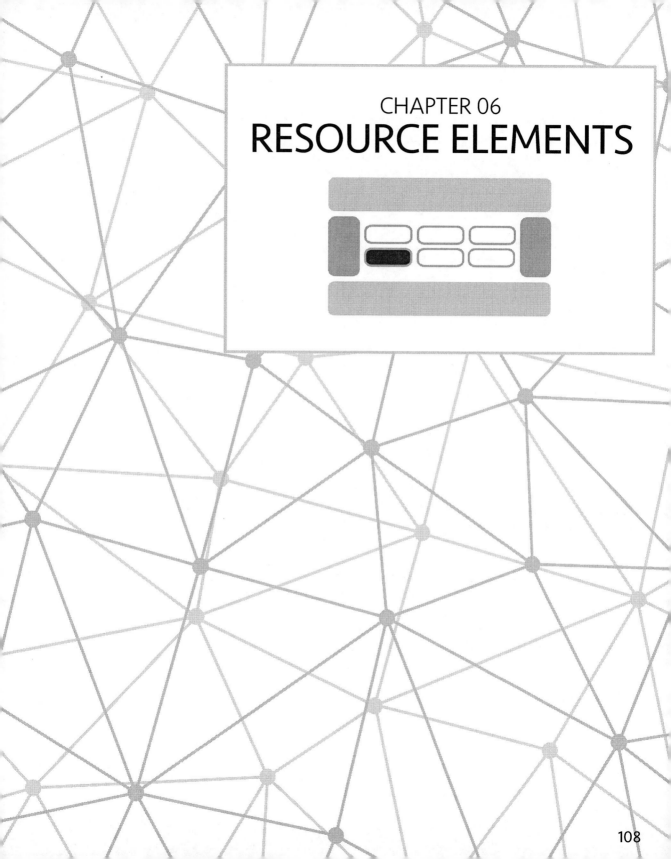

CHAPTER 06
RESOURCE ELEMENTS

Introduction

Resource capacity and competence reflect in the productivity of individuals and groups. Resourceful people tend to get more done with a given body of resources, and by resources, we mean hard and soft assets. More done with a given amount of time. More done with a given amount of capital. More done with a given level of staffing, or process support or technical support. More done with connections, talent and operating systems. Resource capacity and adaptation leads to comparative advantage.

We can view resource capacity and competence in a vast array of roles and functions. The productivity of a research lab focused on discovering the answer to disease pathways. The productivity of supply chains in creating strategic and economic value for customers and supplier alike. The productivity of account teams as they engage and serve relationships with customers and channel partners. The capacity of nonprofits in general. These and many other examples speak to the essence of impact with a given resource base.

Resource capacity and competence is built from system design and experience. Systems are shaped and focused in collections of energy and practical nodes and links. Those help organizations create and capture value. Resourceful teams win more and sustain themselves better because they morph to tackle the ever-changing requirements of their stakeholders. Experience powers resource capacity through scale and scope, spark and savvy, connecting new and old systems along with plain old effort and resilience.

CONSIDER:
[The Power of Full Engagement, Schwartz and Loehr]
[Mental Models, Wagonfoot]
[Making Work Visible, DeGrandis]
[The Arsenal of Democracy, Baime]

Key Areas - Resource

Resource capacity and competence can be examined in terms of management systems and leadership practices that bring out the best in groups and individuals with:

- **Everyday Management Systems**
  - *Order and arrangement, control and administrative balance*

- **Systems Approach and Design**
  - *The orientation of elements, networks and system interfaces/links*

- **Asset Considerations and Usage**
  - *People, time, processes, capital, knack and connections that save*

- **Constraints and Boundaries**
  - *Bottlenecks, barriers, pathways, methods and challenges to progress-making*

- **The Foundations of Persistence**
  - *Perseverance, drive, grit, resilience and the power of grinding*

These are the natural drivers of resource capacity and capability, and they apply in vastly different ways across the landscape of organizations. How individuals and groups evolve into more or less resourceful entities may spell the difference between success and failure, improvement or displacement, innovation or corrosion. Resource capacity impacts our planning options and our decision making, our sense of risk management and our approach to and effectiveness in problem solving, with challenges large and small.

Further Detail - Resource

Resource capacity can be further explored along these lines, and we can open up the assessment with a deeper look into everyday resource thinking. The differences in competing entities is heavily influenced by resource capacity and competence.

Everyday Management Systems

When organizations design their management systems, they are defining what matters and how they arrange and organize the work that deals with what matters. Priorities, standards and approaches are shaped by the resources that make things happen well and consistently. What are the key systems in place that deal with priorities and resources? What is the role of operating and capital budgets? How are exceptions treated? How are opportunities addressed? What is the power of our systems to make us sharp, or dull our efforts? How are these systems governed?

Systems Approach and Design

We have observed systems and processes that make individuals, groups and entire organizations very focused and productive. We have also observed organizations whose systems brought them to their knees with process swamps, bureaucracy and other tensions. Not surprisingly, many organizations would prefer to start over with systems and structures that are designed to manage core business plans, and adjacent or new/next business play in different ways.

CONSIDER:
[Deep Work and Digital Minimalism, Newport]
[Great at Work, Hansen]
[Time, Talent and Energy, Mankins and Garton]

Asset Considerations and Usage

Organizations vary a great deal when it comes to resource leverage and their range of operational assets. Some are quite successful in cranking-up the scale and scope of operations to drive strategic and economic impact. Others are focused on adaptive models and niche approaches to building comparative advantage and economic sustenance. How does the management team put the focus on asset usage and resource leverage in a way that responds to near-term objectives and long-term options? How do we manage scope and scale? How are these many assets governed? What about sustainability?

Constraints and Boundaries

Resources can be constrained by many things. Not enough people. Not enough time. Not enough data, knowledge or insight. Not enough experience or process capability. Not enough scale or scope. Not enough research. Not enough operating capacity or supply chain capacity or channel capacity. And then there are matters of leadership and management and the constraints we associate with order and guidance in the field or in the lab. Constraints are everywhere, so how do we address them in ways that enable and engage our teams to succeed?

CONSIDER:
[Creating a Lean Culture, Mann]
[Hitchhikers Guide to Lean, Flinchbaugh and Carlino]
[When: Secrets of Perfect Timing, Pink]
[Lean Solutions, Womack and Jones]
[Scale and Scope: Industrial Capitalism, Chandler]
[Lean Enterprise, Humble, Molesky and O'Reilly]

The Ethics of Persistence

Persistence matters to workers, students, researchers, athletes, artists, parents, executives, technicians and just about everybody else, and in every walk of life. Persistence is built in courage and confidence, resilience and passion, and the push to overcome. We persist to discover and comply. We press to achieve and realize and drive outcomes. We persist to improve and innovate. What kind of persistence brings out the best in people regardless of constraints and barriers? What kind of thought and behavior do we see in our most persistent teams? What about patience?

CONSIDER:
[GRIT: The Power of Passion/Perseverance, Duckworth]

Resourceful people get things done against the odds, in remarkable ways, sometimes with very clever ways and means. They find ways to collaborate when working separately is not a workable option. They accept the tensions of distraction, and they stay on-focus despite the noise. They deal with the politics of accountability while marching through the inevitable smoke and haze of getting things done, of executing well.

Resourceful people get work done on-track and on-time. They power project integration and process making because they engage in things with curiosity, urgency, influence and courage. They understand the paradox of work that presses for compliance at the same time it presses for discovery. Resource savvy is intentional, sparked by the ability to adapt. Resource savvy leaders are highly-engaged and driven.

CONSIDER:
[X-Teams, Bresman and Ancona]
[Design for Operational Excellence, Duggan]
[Time, Talent and Energy, Mankins and Garton]

Development Considerations

Resource competence and capacity is learned and developed in a range of experiences, many of which are informal but powerful. There are formal and more structured lessons in resource management as well. These emerge from system study and simulation, and practice and experimentation. All of this leads to important questions in four areas:

- ***Leadership and Management View***
  - *What matters, and why is resource competence important?*

- ***Common Indicators and Criteria***
  - *What are the practical markers of resource competence?*

- ***Experiential Learning Approach and Focus***
  - *What is the roadmap for resource capacity and competence?*

- ***Connecting with the Other Elements***
  - *What makes resource competence relevant to our team roles?*

Almost everyone has a role that operates on resource capacity in some way, and in some context. Almost everyone lives with input-output tensions that force them to balance time and attention. Many of us have plans to manage, decisions to make, risks to balance and problems to solve and we have natural constraints in resources, and natural barriers to navigate. Some of us eat priority lists for breakfast. Some of us anticipate obstacles. Some of us adapt easily to change. Some of us discover extra time and capacity every day. Some of us stretch budgets, energy and practice to power superior efforts, and results. These traits are essential in team development, and organization development.

Leadership and Management View

Resource capability starts with individuals and operates through groups of people serving in teams and collective roles. Getting the right things done with the resources provided or available is a big piece of the management and leadership equation in every endeavor. How do we set the tone for resource use and productivity? What resource tools and methods are appropriate for getting to objectives, dealing with challenges, resolving problems, making progress? What sparks individual hearts and minds to press-on regardless? What happens when project resources run low, or run dry? How do we adapt and change?

CONSIDER:
[Smarter Faster Better, Duhigg]

Common Indicators and Criteria

What does effective resource capacity leverage and performance mean for organizations and those who depend on outputs, support and services? What kind of markers and progress measures do we assign? What are the gauges that matter most? What about process compliance? What about system capacity? What about adaptive capability or improvisation, or going without critical resources in mission critical work? What kind of shared Learning and Development pathways do we have in place for our people and for emerging teams? What value creation and capture themes apply with resource capacity and competence?

CONSIDER:
[Keeping Score, Brown]
[Measure Up, Lynch and Cross]
[Bullseye!, Schiemann and Lingle]

Experiential Learning Approach and Focus

Resource skills and savvy are learned in structured discipline and practice with systems, and through experience and dynamic exercise. Basic skills that power our attention and contextual thinking are important foundations. We have to understand and appreciate what we gather through our landscape lenses before we can fully engage in resource leverage. But what kinds of experience really drive us in the acquisition of resource capacity and capability? What experiments, challenges, lab exercises, long marches, case work and improv tests are meaningful as we seek to match our resource savvy? What kind of experience makes for clever, savvy, faster, smarter, better teams and individuals? Who is curious about this?

Connecting with the Other Elements

Resource capacity and competence relates to each and every use of the working elements that individuals and teams depend on – technical, analytic, creative, solution and relational. We need resource capacity in everybody, and teams perform on the energy of resource capacity. What is the magic synapse between resource capacity and creative capacity, or resource capacity and analytic capacity? When organizations are faced with major challenges or super-wicked problems, what is the significance of resource capacity? How do individuals with a sixth sense of resource savvy bring out the very best in others? Who makes connections?

CONSIDER:
[The Process Edge, Keen]
[Hyperfocus: The Productivity Project, Bailey]

Check Points - Resource

Individuals shape team effort and performance with their talent and their perspective. Those with reserves of resource capacity and competence are essential on teams that are responsible for growth, performance and change. Resource leverage is key to strategy integration and execution.

Intentional Questions ...
Purpose, Roles, Challenges, Risks

What is the kind of resource capacity and competence that goes with key roles in the organization? What does resource leverage mean in the context of different kinds of work? How do resource-savvy leaders influence the culture of the organization? How do teams balance urgency, diligence, procrastination, patience, resolve?

Standard Diagnostics ...
Thoughts on Assessment and Evaluation

Specific assessments for resource compliance are the domain of other practices, but we can ask the questions, how do we gauge the resource capacity of individuals and groups in the organization? How can we tell? How do we gather the assurance that people are suited-up for challenges? What do we expect and how can they perform?

Developmental Guidelines ...
Learning/Development

Resource capacity is partly innate and mostly learned, meaning that some people come to their roles with a keen sense of priorities and resources and others are less naturally inclined. From the start, we gain insight with regard to resource leverage, systems, stretch performance, dealing with constraints, moving the bar, mastering resolve and impact.

Engaging ...
Standard, Powerful, Effective and Savvy

Resource capacity reflects in strategy, culture and structure, through the routine thought and behavior of individuals and teams. Almost everybody has been exposed to practice and methods, technique and process. Whether perfect is the objective, or whether excellence and progress are the formula markers, organizations with "**resource edge**" are better.

More Detail, in Context

Moving the Learning and Development agenda forward, we can address some of the most common resource issues and considerations that unfold in most organizations.

Intentional Questions ...
Purpose, Roles, Challenges, Risks

Resource capacity and competence shapes how individuals and groups behave relative to tasks, processes, and roles. This is a big piece of the organization's culture relative to growth, performance and change. How and why does resource capacity impact the comparative advantage of the enterprise, or our ability to serve customers, or our financial performance and sustenance? Why is resource capacity so relevant to every level of the organization, down to the front lines? Where does the message of resource capacity resonate?

Standard Diagnostics ...
Thoughts on Assessment and Evaluation

While there are evaluation platforms that address resource capacity for almost every enterprise, assessments must be matched with action and experience to generate a measure of capability. What do individuals and teams get done under pressure? How do different people respond when things hit the fan? How well do teams realign and redeploy themselves when the "change orders" start to cascade? These are **action measures** that may reflect in standard assessments. What we measure may be situation-specific or more general in nature. What gets our attention when things evolve?

CONSIDER:
[How We Work, Weiss]
[Leading Agile Teams, Rose]
[The Agile Mind-Set, Broza]
[The Knowledge Work Factory, Heitman]

Developmental Guidelines ...
Learning/Development

Resource capacity often parallels analytic capacity when it comes to Learning and Development pathways. Certain aspects of resource capacity and competence are open to experiential learning and stimulation, and we can cite examples from bridge construction to surgical procedures, where doing something under practice conditions is valuable and may be perfectable. Much of the world is subject to cumulative and dynamic experience, under different circumstances and with different performance criteria. How do we cultivate the appropriate resource sense and sensitivity with our people and our teams? What can the different generations and genders learn from one another?

Engaging ...
Standard, Powerful, Effective and Savvy

Engagement means a lot with resource capacity. It reflects on commitment and focus and discretionary effort. It revolves on spirit and challenge and adaptation. It steps up to accountability, and it takes responsibility. How is resource capacity something that lives and dies on the back of individual and group engagement? Why do some people choose to be sluggards who are unable to answer the call with resource capacity and competence? How does gifted leadership push the bar on experience-based practice, in and across the organization; and further, is this really a good idea, or just a cliché? And finally, an idea, **give the really big tasks to your really busy people**.

What does resource capacity provide the individual, the team and the broader organization? How do we acquire the talent we really need vis-à-vis resource savvy and sense? How do we intervene when there are gaps in resource capacity? Who has the responsibility for resource capacity and competence across the span of organizational assets and talent?

CONSIDER:
[Scrum Project Management, Metcalfe]
[Project Management for the Unofficial Project Manager, Kogon, Blakemore, Wood]
[The Work of a Project Team, Peters]

Summary – Resource Elements

Resource capacity is a defining factor across most organizations, and for most individuals. Resource capacity is personal and professional in nature. Resource capacity is complex, situation-specific and dynamic. It defines why we target priorities, how we appropriate time and effort, what we measure, and who is on the line for efforts and outcomes. Resource capacity and competence is at the heart of individual and team productivity, and relative productivity is a key factor in the evolution and sustenance of every organization.

Resource capacity is not just about time or capital or task management, and the overall resource picture is often too murky to measure. Resources are sometimes tangible and obvious, but often they are soft and intangible. What really matters is **resource leverage**– getting the right kind of effort and results from the resources we have available, in the context of the challenges and constraints that come with the situation. Things are just as simple and difficult as that.

Think about:

- *The key areas of resource capacity*

- *How these contribute to team capacity*

- *How these complement other Talent Blocks*

- *The targets of team/resource development*

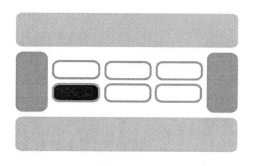

Summary Audit: Resource Capacity

Introduction

Organizations have diverse needs and requirements for Resource Capacity, and they also have different approaches to Learning and Development. The intent of this summary audit of Resource Capacity is simply to connect some themes for gauging the relevance, applications and measures that go with Resource Capacity. This audit approach can be modified to match the interests and requirements of the organization with talent development pathways that make the most sense for individuals and teams.

Resource Capacity and Competence

- ***Everyday Management Systems***

  General Considerations …
     - situations, challenges

  Development Considerations …
     - alternatives, horizons

- ***Systems Approach and Design***

  General Considerations …
     - situations, challenges

  Development Considerations …
     - alternatives, horizons

- ***Assets Considerations and Usage***

  General Considerations ...
  - *situations, challenges*

  Development Considerations ...
  - *alternatives, horizons*

- ***Constraints and Boundaries***

  General Considerations ...
  - *situations, challenges*

  Development Considerations ...
  - *alternatives, horizons*

- ***The Foundations of Persistence***

  General Considerations ...
  - *situations, challenges*

  Development Considerations ...
  - *alternatives, horizons*

Collective Impact and Implications

Near-Term and Long-Term Themes

Notebook

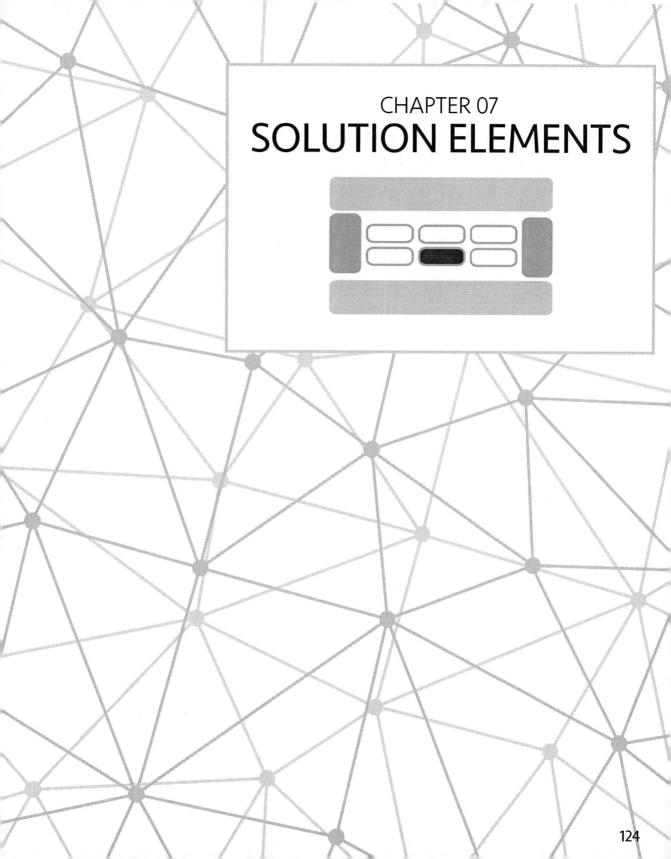

CHAPTER 07
SOLUTION ELEMENTS

Introduction

Solution capacity and competence are framed in our approach to problems and how we deal with them. We develop the knack to identify and resolve problems in different ways. Experience is a great teacher in this arena. People with strong solution skills bring everyday thought and behavior that is key to team performance.

Solution skills play out in every organization, in a broad range of tasks, relationships and roles. Development roles such as Research demand deep solution thinking. Integration roles in operations and field management are dependent on matching solutions with existing and emerging problems in the heat of action. Compliance roles balance problems with solutions, with rules and mandates, standards, protocols and constraints.

Solution sense and skills are learned from method and experience. We gather solution capacity from study in scientific method and games, and through formulaic practice with processes. We learn about solution thinking in everyday work, everyday play, everyday adaptation to conditions, events, challenges and barriers. Education is a journey of finding problems and solving them, in standard ways, and new ways.

CONSIDER:
[Decisive, Heath and Heath]
[The Opposable Mind, Martin]
[The Art of Problem Posing, Brown and Walter]
[How to Think Like Leonardo da Vinci, Gelb]

Key Areas - Solution

The nature of solution capacity and competence can be defined in terms that reflect across five areas, referenced below and in the following pages.

- ***Challenge Lenses***
  - *Cutting through the clutter to find the root cause of problems, challenges*

- ***Everyday, Basic Problems***
  - *The frame for systematic and faster routing problem resolution*

- ***Extended, Complex Problems***
  - *The frame for deeper, network-savvy problem assessment, resolution*

- ***Super-Wicked Problem Sets***
  - *The frame for managing components, parts, subsystems and complexity*

- ***Evolution Lenses***
  - *Managing Dual-Dynamic horizons, scenario models, change practice*

These five areas of solution capacity and competence shape how we come to deal with the **identification, prevention, mitigation, resolution and recovery from problems** in everyday work and everyday life. All kinds of problems, business and personal, economic and political, cultural and societal, operating and strategic are subject to this capacity track.

Further Detail - Solution

We can take a look at the essence of each of these areas, exploring the scope and nature of solution methods and practices in more depth. We can pose questions that advance the view of solution management and governance.

Challenge Lenses and Focus

When we look at our challenges, large and small, we tend to define them in terms we can tackle and solve. How can we best map our field of challenges, our minefield of especially big and tough challenges? How can we generate alternative views of our challenges, different perspectives, different angles and different structures? How can we be sure to define the right problem sets and context? These are starting point questions for solution management. These help establish the solution frame with common sense.

Everyday, Basic Problems

Some problems are routine. They recur and repeat. Everyday basic problems have patterns and pathways that are relatively simple to discern and tag. What can we do to corral, understand, mitigate and prevent everyday, simple problems? What can we do to automate or accelerate basic problem solving processes? How could we just ignore some basic problems and let them just die from exposure? These questions set us up to keep little problems from becoming big problems. Basic communication?

CONSIDER:
[Exploring the Scientific Method, Gimbel]

Extended, Complex Problems

Some problems are more complex, and more interwoven. There are problems that have multiple sources and causes, sometimes multiple influences, competing interests and tensions in play. Unlike routine problems with relatively simple approaches to resolution, complex problems tend to require unique and specific answers. What about fielding the right definition of the problem? What about the discernment of the right solution against the objectives of the enterprise? What about framing the value and presumed risks of the best solution?

Super-Wicked Problem Sets

Some problems are so complicated, so complex that they probably cannot be solved as a whole. Or, maybe they can be solved as a whole, but not with a singular solution. The technical, social and economic tensions of Healthcare Reform frame a special kind of super-wicked problem. World peace and justice have some super-wickedness in play. What is the right starting point for dealing with these problems? What kind of leadership and management covers this kind of territory? Who defines the elements to address?

CONSIDER:
[Think In Systems, McKey]
[Cracked It! Problems and Solutions, Phelps]
[Farsighted, Johnson]
[Sprint: Solve Problems, Knapp]
[The Systems Thinker, Rutherford]
[Wicked Problems and Social Complexity, Conklin]

Evolution Lenses, Horizons

Most organizations operate in a world that is, at some level and in some form, **VUCA ... volatile, uncertain, complex and ambiguous**. Anticipating the nature of our unfolding horizons is a kind of solution work, looking ahead, plotting what conditions may emerge, converge or diverge. Solution work involves thinking through scenarios to understand, adapt and simulate our plans. What issues and problems are on the horizon? How does the organization get things in scope? What is future-readiness all about? How do individuals and teams gear-up to embrace the nature of current and future state problems? Attention?

CONSIDER:
[Quantum Leadership, Porter-O'Grady and Malloch]

Solution management is a broad arena for individuals and groups. We have the dual task of dealing with both big and small problems as everyday work. How we deal with problems may represent a significant point of competitive advantage. Dealing with problems could involve a breakthrough discovery that is a game-changer. Dealing with simple and complex problems in some new and systematic manner could make an organization better, smarter and faster than its competitive peers. So again, we ask ourselves, how can we make solution capacity and competence the difference-maker? How do we engage solution competence? How does this bake into culture?

CONSIDER:
[Only the Paranoid Survive, Grove]
[Next is Now, Arussy]

Development Considerations

Solution capacity and competence is generally learned in method and in routine practice, with experience, and with more practice. How we recognize problems in context, how we see our pathways to resolution and how we frame problems and challenges to be resolved are subject to building our solution mindset with:

- ***Leadership and Management View***
    - *What matters, and why is solution competence important?*

- ***Common Indicators and Criteria***
    - *What are the practical markers of solution competence?*

- ***Experiential Learning Approach and Focus***
    - *What is the roadmap for solution capacity and competence?*

- ***Connecting with the Other Elements***
    - *What makes solution competence relevant to our roles?*

Most of us work in roles that require problem recognition, prevention, mitigation, resolution and readiness. **High-Reliability Organizations** in the military and in healthcare take a cultural and focused approach to solution capacity and competence. Research organizations and seed acceleration teams take a systematic and exploratory approach. Educators, mentors, parents and coaches take a developmental, often sequential approach to solution Learning and Development. Some of us are problem scouts. Some of us are problem preventers. Some of us are tasked with managing cumulative problems. Some of us are designated problem killers. Some of us are on the clean-up crew, for problem solving and recovery.

Leadership and Management View

How does a group or team set about developing solution capacity and competence? What are the key ingredients? What is the process? Who sets the practice? What kind of discipline is necessary for solving problems large and small? Who inspires everyday solution work, specialized solution work, robust and urgent solution work? What about future problems? What about building the capacity to solve undefined, emergent problems with innovative, adaptive solutions? What about prevention, intervention, compliance, discovery and recovery?

Common Indicators and Criteria

What is the most basic level of the most essential kind of solution sense we need with our people? What makes some people better solution makers than others and what can we do to identify, cultivate, engage and disperse that ability? What are the common barriers to solution capacity, and do we have what we need to deal with constraints? What is the strategic, operating and economic value of solution capacity, fast and slow, sharp and dull, better and worse? What really matters, and why? What gets in the way of solution capacity? Who really cares?

Experiential Learning Approach and Focus

Much of our capacity to solve problems is learned through direct experience and practice. Even when method and technique are essential, practice is *more* essential. We learn to anticipate, to connect, to sense progress and danger, to frame and craft answers. We learn by trial and error, success and failure, victory and defeat. The key questions are always there. How do we solve challenges, puzzles and complex problems? What do we bring to the horns of a dilemma? How do we pass down our solution sense to our "youngers" and how do they bring it to their respective "elders" in the organization of diverse stakeholders?

Connecting with the Other Elements

Solution capacity is a dynamic part of our individual, group and community expression of capability. It goes with our technical, analytic, creative, resource and relational capacity to shape who we are and what we bring to our tasks and roles. Some of us appear as Worker Bee agents of routine solution efforts. What enables some of us to appear as "Rainman" savants who, somehow, just come up with answers and solutions to stuff we may not even recognize as a challenge or problem? What makes some of us able to serve as powerful breeder-reactors for ideas and solutions to complex challenges? Communication?

CONSIDER:
[Driven By Difference, Livermore]
[Collaborative Intelligence, Markova and McArthur]
[The Diversity Bonus, Page]

Check Points - Solution

We need check points that help us gauge the "right stuff" in solution work, the right methods, the right kind of thought and behavior. We also need the consideration of alternative views, opposable minds, continuous tracks, differential sense. These contribute to a richer formula for cultivating the everyday effects of people making strategy happen.

Intentional Questions ...
Purpose, Roles, Challenges, Risks

What is the nature and scope of solution capacity and competence required of the individual role and the organization as a whole? What does solution capacity mean for stakeholders? How does solution capacity factor in to the successful evolution, performance, progress and sustenance of the enterprise?

Standard Diagnostics ...
Thoughts on Assessment and Evaluation

There are some interesting ways to test for solution smarts and broader problem solving capacity, but for the purposes of this FieldBook, we are agnostic about specific assessments. However, it's always a good idea to build a bench of solution makers, hackers, explorers, servers and feeders. What specific and general markers are meaningful?

Developmental Guidelines ...
Learning/Development

Solution capacity appears in different forms, with different people who exercise their gifts in different ways and means. Every individual and group deserves a roadmap that provides at least some guidance about problems, solutions and solution-building practice. That map should be powered by activity-based learning.

Engaging ...
Standard, Powerful, Effective and Savvy

Engagement is part focus and motivation, part deliberate effort, part fierce commitment and part accountability for results. Across the elements, deep and abiding engagement in solution capacity can make huge differences, life and death differences in the work of an organization. Engagement in solution management is part of basic training, or should be.

More Detail, in Context

Breaking things down further, we can push the theory and practice of solution capacity into a host of managerial probes and questions that serve to guide Learning and Development.

Intentional Questions ...
Purpose, Roles, Challenges, Risks

"Why bother with solution capacity – every organization has problems and they eventually get resolved." That statement marks the graveyards of organizations, project teams and joint ventures. Successful individual groups and organizations exist to solve challenges. Otherwise, how would they generate new strategic and economic value? In different settings and circumstances, what does solution capacity really mean for stakeholders – customers, employers, investors, partners, suppliers? What is the consequence of weak solution capacity? What are the benefits of looking at how others tackle problems?

Standard Diagnostics ...
Thoughts on Assessment and Evaluation

Educators at the Pre-K/12 and Higher Education levels speak about the importance of individual and group problem solving. They prescribe methods and markers for matching approaches to solutions and the caliber of the solutions themselves. One kind of solution marker is an answer to a problem. Another kind of solution marker is a discovery, or insight or expression that defines and addresses the problem-solution process. What about measures of routine, simple problem solving? What about measures of complex problem solving or super-wicked problem set parsing? What about solution speed, quality, leverage, advantage, durability, application and forward prevention?

Developmental Guidelines ...
Learning/Development

We are exposed at an early and curious stage to solving problems, solving puzzles, and dealing with the mazes we are surrounded with. We gain the capacity to sense problems and see challenges and gauge tensions that need resolution. We learn our way into solution capacity and competence with standard lessons, study models, case practice, unstructured projects and play. How do we build solution capacity and discipline, technique and process, readiness and resolve? Without Learning and Development pathways, solution capacity and competence emerge at random. Maybe that is good enough, but how do we make it work?

Engaging ...
Standard, Powerful, Effective and Savvy

Highly engaged solution crafters are typically prospective, thoughtful, often relentless and obsessive, connected, sometimes open to arguments. They are often focused on a mind track of unfettered effort and persistence. How is **solution attention** a product of practice and sometimes a product of forward sense and field of vision? How do we engage deeply and broadly at the same time, with lateral and vertical lenses and filters for our thinking? How do we curate solutions in small, highly focused chambers of thinking and doing?

CONSIDER:
[Adaptive Enterprise, Haeckel]
[Extended Enterprise, Davis and Spekman]

How does the culture of an organization reflect on the solution capacities and competencies of the individuals who make up that organization? How do we, as individuals, cast our roles against the tasks and expectations of our stakeholders in search of solutions? How do those solutions accrue into strategic and economic value? Are we truly intentional about solution capacity and competence? How do we get more contemplative and serious here?

135

Summary – Solution Elements

Solution capacity, perspective, attention, engagement and competence are parts of the formula for growth, performance and change-regardless of the nature of the organization. Problems appear in different forms, and sometimes they appear in clouds of mystery, risk and wonder. Solution capacity enables individuals and teams to master, avoid and reduce problems, and it gives an organization the power for navigation. We also need to understand the basics of problem recovery and solution integration, and the art of getting better.

Solutions are sometimes pure and formulaic. Sometimes solutions are not all that clear; they may be imperfect and unbalanced and even the source of other problems. Solution capacity ties to standard processes, situations, circumstances, readiness, crazy luck, persistence, character, engagement, knack and, for some, the power of faith. Solutions are easy, and difficult, routine and unique, cheap and expensive. Solutions make the game interesting.

Think about:

- *The key areas of solution capacity*

- *How these contribute to team capacity*

- *How these complement other Talent Blocks*

- *The targets of team/solution development*

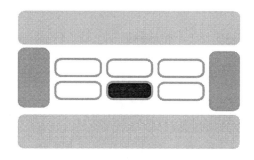

Summary Audit: Solution Capacity

Introduction

Organizations have diverse needs and requirements for Solution Capacity, and they also have different approaches to Learning and Development. The intent of this summary audit of Solution Capacity is simply to connect some themes for gauging the relevance, applications and measures that go with Solution Capacity. This audit approach can be modified to match the interests and requirements of the organization with talent development pathways that make the most sense to individuals and teams.

Solution Capacity and Competence

- ***Challenge Lenses***

    General Considerations ...
    - *situations, challenges*

    Development Considerations ...
    - *alternatives, horizons*

- ***Everyday, Basic Problems***

    General Considerations ...
    - *situations, challenges*

    Development Considerations ...
    - *alternatives, horizons*

- **Extended, Complex Problems**

  General Considerations …
  - *situations, challenges*

  Development Considerations …
  - *alternatives, horizons*

- **Super-Wicked Problem Sets**

  General Considerations …
  - *situations, challenges*

  Development Considerations …
  - *alternatives, horizons*

- **Evolution Lenses**

  General Considerations …
  - *situations, challenges*

  Development Considerations …
  - *alternatives, horizons*

Collective Impact and Implications

Near-Term and Long-Term Themes

Notebook

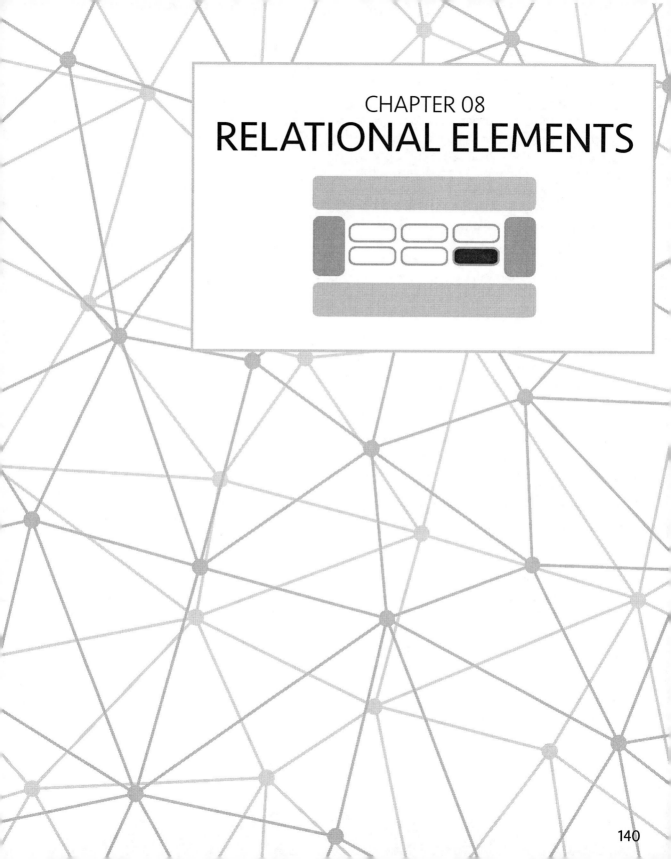

CHAPTER 08
RELATIONAL ELEMENTS

Introduction

Relational capacity and competence are shaped in the way people see each other, work together, serve each other, engage together, and make each other better. We develop relational sense and sustenance in personal terms, and broader social terms, through experience. People with very strong relational skills appear to spark teams and groups to do their best, although the opposite can drive behaviors as well.

We can view relational capacity and competence in different roles and applications, and those may include project teams, customer support, operating groups, governing boards, front line processes, back room functions, stakeholder functions and many other streams of activity. Anywhere people work together in some fashion or manner, relational skills are part of the picture. Individuals with demonstrated levels of awareness, empathy, attention, political sense and self-governance are products of higher relational capacity and competence. At the other end of the spectrum, the lack of these attributes can seriously disrupt, and perhaps even destroy relationships.

Relational ability is a function of character, study and experience. Relational skills are informed by persona, sharpened in both positive and negative exposure with others, built on a body of integrated Learning and Development. Relational capacity is part emotional intelligence, part interpersonal sensitivity, part individual confidence and respect. Relationships are engineered by people, and people make strategy happen by working effectively with other people, with and through the power of effective relationships.

CONSIDER:
[Friend of a Friend, Burkus]
[Drive: Motivation, Pink]
[Care to Lead, McGalliard]
[Designing the Smart Organization, Deiser]

Key Areas - Relational

For individuals, teams and organizations as a whole, the definition of relational capacity and competence can be explored under the following points:

- **Everyday Leadership, Action**
  - *Sensing, guiding and serving relationships with other individuals and groups*

- **Perspective and Attention**
  - *Gathering the big picture, working the small details, and everything in between*

- **Personal Awareness and Confidence**
  - *Reflection, appreciation, social focus, persistence, compassion, awareness*

- **Situational Judgment and Sense**
  - *Knowledge, understanding, contextual wisdom and savvy, environment*

- **Deeper Trust and Credibility**
  - *Essential, confident trust and human reliability; power, energy, service*

These are the touch stones of relational capacity and competence, and they occur in the stream of all kinds of personal exchanges and interactions. They reflect in great relationships with colleagues, friends and connections. They also reflect in our most difficult interactions, with challenging issues and deplorable people that test us.

CONSIDER:
[Influencer: Grenny, Patterson, McMillan, Maxfield, Switzler]
[Influence Without Authority, Cohen and Bradford]
[Contagious: Why Things Catch On, Berger]

Further Detail - Relational

We need to explore each of these dimensions of relational capacity and competence in terms that are relevant to us at a personal level. There are several important questions that go with this element.

Everyday Leadership

Understanding how and why people interact is a starting point for effective leadership. What do they need in order to function and perform? Why do they engage with one another? How do they make choices and deal with tensions, priorities, goals and setbacks? These and other questions are part of the leadership formula that connects our expectations, behavior and performance. And ... leadership at every level.

CONSIDER:
[Big Potential, Achor]
[Act Like a Leader, Think Like a Leader, Ibarra]
[Social: Brains Wired to Connect, Lieberman]

Perspective and Attention

Across the organization and under different conditions, what do we really see and sense? How do we gather and arrange insights? What draws our attention and focus, and what do we miss? The world is rich with noise and distractions, and cutting through the clutter to sense what matters, what is real, what is meaningful is a big piece of the relational capacity and competence puzzle. Check, are we missing anything?

CONSIDER:
[You Are the Team, Rogers]
[Supportive Accountability, Melena]
[Five Languages of Appreciation, Chapman and White]

Personal Awareness and Confidence

Self-awareness is an essential building block for relational capacity. Social awareness and the contextual senses that go with our broader cultural, political and systemic views support how well we can gather and shape insights. What keeps us open to ideas, relationships and change? What keeps us resilient to the tensions and conflicts that naturally come with relationships? What is the roadmap for getting to confidence - in confidence alone?

CONSIDER:
[Multipliers, Wiseman]
[Get Better, Davis]
[Leading the Unleadable, Willett]
[In Defense of Troublemakers, Nemeth]

Situational Judgment and Sense

How we gauge risks and opportunities depends on judgment, and how well our personal sensors and radar work. How well do we observe and explore issues and conditions? How can we make snap judgments under stress without blowing the game? How can we make sense of things by disciplined observation and orientation, setting the stage for orderly decision making and action? Where does good judgment come from? Experience ... and evolution from poor judgment. Situational awareness and savvy count.

CONSIDER:
[Work Rules!, Bock]
[Judgment, Tichy and Bennis]
[Applied Empathy, Ventura]
[That's What She Said, Lipman]

Deeper Trust and Credibility

Human trust is the critical bond that enables individuals, groups and organizations to work together, live together and serve together. Trust is catalytic in so many aspects of relational capacity. Reliability, consistency, dependability and respectability are part of the trust equation. At some level, faith in the service and efforts of others, the broader plan and the greater power make people credible and worthy of trust with one another. How does trust come together? How does the bridge of trust, knowledge and power come together for individuals and teams? Communicate!

CONSIDER:
[Trusted Partners, Lewis]
[Managing By Defining Moments, Meredith and Schewe]

People interact with each other in settings that post challenges and choices, priorities and constraints, influences and cultural forces. Somehow, people get things done. They collaborate, more or less effectively. They develop ideas and exchange views, with better systematic and respectful efforts, or not. They settle conflicts and press on with the journey; maybe they struggle. Relational capacity is something that engages individuals and teams together and in common cause, as people making strategy happen.

CONSIDER:
[Radical Trust, Healey]
[Social Physics, Pentland]
[Score!, Conflict to Collaboration, Stallkamp]
[Extraordinary Influence, Irwin]

Development Considerations

Relational capacity and competence is learned behavior that is shaped by some natural elements of personality and expression. Developing the relational capacity of individuals and groups is supported by deliberate engagement across four areas:

- **Leadership and Management View**
  - *What matters, and why is relational competence important?*

- **Common Indicators and Criteria**
  - *What are the practical markers of relational competence?*

- **Experiential Learning Approach and Focus**
  - *What is the roadmap for relational capacity and competence?*

- **Connecting with the Other Elements**
  - *What makes relational competence relevant to our roles?*

Most of us need to function well as individuals, and together in groups, project teams, departments, social settings, family systems, communities and all kinds of organizations and communal systems. Some of us have leadership roles that demand our powers of influence and our foundations of trust. Some of us are operatives, working together in relationships where we are expected to function with or without effective leadership. Some of us work with jerks. Some of us are recovering jerks. Some of us are full of grace and relational sense serving those we work with.

Leadership and Management View

Who sets the stage for relational competence and culture, and who defines what is appropriate and engaging behavior among and between individuals? What are the table stakes for good interpersonal communication, exchange, connection and team engagement? What are the "centering" methods and devices we use to gather perspectives, insights and concerns? What are the standards and practices we use to address conflicts, barriers, challenges and options? How do we lead change?

CONSIDER:
[The Individualized Corporation, Ghoshal and Bartlett]
[The Transparent Leader, Baum]
[The Will to Lead, Bower]
[The Leadership Engine, Tichy]

Common Indicators and Criteria

How would we distinguish between a group of people who function really well together and perform consistently well at high levels, from a group that struggles with everything they do? What are the measures of relational capacity and perspective, attention, judgment, awareness, resilience and trust? What is our tolerance for difficult people and backward groups? What does conflict confrontation and resolution look like? What is the gauge of emotional and social intelligence in our organization? Do our people adapt well, sense well, serve well?

Experiential Learning Approach and Focus

Into the mix of relational capacity and competence goes at least some stuff from our innate selves, our curious DNA and makeup. However, most of our capacity for effective relational operation comes from experience. That may be formal Learning and Development experience, and experience with duty under stress, experience with really effective leaders and managers, experience with positive and negative influences, and on it goes. What does experience teach us about the nature and borders of relational capacity and competence? Can we formalize the process of relational capacity for Learning and Development?

CONSIDER:
[Wired to Care, Patnaik]
[Experiential Learning, Kolb]
[Adaptive Leadership, Heifetz, Linsky and Grashow]

Connecting with the Other Elements

Relational capacity is a connector, and it provides a lot of the exchange network that interfaces with our respective technical, analytic, creative, resource and solution capacities. Some of us with high-functioning relational skills are especially effective at bringing people together to address challenges, objectives, discovery and integration work. Others use their relational capabilities to navigate and negotiate, inform and influence, engage others and advance the purpose they serve. What is the difference? How do we connect and adapt? What do we exchange with other people whose strengths complement our assets?

CONSIDER:
[Leading Outside the Lines, Katzenbach and Khan]

Check Points - Relational

As we examine our individual and collective purpose, there are some things that need our highest relational attention. There are lenses through which we view how different people work together or in isolation to get things done, to connect, deal with issues and prosper.

Intentional Questions ...
Purpose, Roles, Challenges, Risks

What kind of relational capacity and competence is prescribed for the nature of the role, the organization, the area of interest? And, what place does relational capacity have in the adaptation of the individual people and organizations?

Standard Diagnostics ...
Thoughts on Assessment and Evaluation

People skills, soft skills, team skills ... these are the subjects of available tests and assessments. They are also table stakes in the measure of individuals working well with others in settings that somehow bring out the best in others.

Developmental Guidelines ...
Learning/Development

Some good fortune colors how people with strong relational capacity and skills seem to come together. For the rest of us, there is some process and culture in play as we attract, cultivate and sustain people who are adept at working together, for impact and purpose.

Engaging ...
Standard, Powerful, Effective and Savvy

Relational skills engage or constrain individuals and groups with respect, empathy, courage, resolve, support, curiosity and influence. Trust lives large in organizations that are, by nature, well-endowed with relational competence and sustaining cultures.

More Detail, in Context

Further details and points of view follow the unfolding conversation on relational skills and everyday thought and behavior. These questions explore interactions and streams of energy.

Intentional Questions ...
Purpose, Roles, Challenges, Risks

Simply put, why do relational skills matter? How do we set expectations for individual and group interaction? What general and specific relational sense and capacity is appropriate in different roles and functions? What real value does relational capacity bring to different situations and settings? Why does this matter to stakeholders? How does this matter to us as individuals? How does this matter to the broader culture?

CONSIDER:
[The Power of Moments, Heath and Heath]
[We Need to Talk: Conversations that Matter, Headlee]

Standard Diagnostics ...
Thoughts on Assessment and Evaluation

Some personality and temperament types are more naturally suited-up with relational capacity and competence. Organizations can assess those attributes and tendencies. The practical markers often come down to the basics of how well we function with others, how we communicate, interact, encourage, influence and serve with purpose. Gauging people skills and soft skills is part of the assessment mix. Gauging how people work under stress and how well they function in different settings is a key Learning and Development theme.

CONSIDER:
[The No Asshole Rule, Sutton]
[The Asshole Survival Guide, Sutton]
[Diagnosing and Changing Culture, Cameron and Quinn]

Developmental Guidelines ...
Learning/Development

Personality differences and attitudinal constructs aside, most of what people bring to the relational skills party is learned from a combination of formal and informal experience. Self-awareness, along with personal regulation are pivotal human development factors. What about social awareness and situation sense are things we establish in our educational experience, team and congregate experience, character training and other activity? What are some of the Learning and Development efforts we make at a purely personal level? What are some of the remedial efforts we make to address what we may have missed in our youth?

CONSIDER:
[The Road to Character, Brooks]
[The Character Gap, Miller]
[Playful Intelligence, DeBenedet]

Engaging ...
Standard, Powerful, Effective and Savvy

High engagement in relational matters is almost always a positive force for good in individuals, groups and organizations. Relational skills are, to a large degree, engagement assets because they help us sort out our purpose and the connections. How do we work with those who share our purpose and tasks, the tools and influences we need to perform, and the trusted partnership we need to be effective? How do we think through the relational issues that touch the "talent button" in every organization? People make strategy happen through relationships, and we need to focus on that premise as we engage others.

How does an individual come to embrace the essential elements of relational capacity and competence? Why does this matter so much across organizations and in the trenches of project management and function integration? What are the tasks of intentional leadership and management relative to relational capacity and competence?

151

Summary – Relational Elements

Relational sense is part of the currency of communication, perspective, judgment, trust and appreciation. For a lot of reasons, relational capacity can be tough to develop and sustain as a cultural asset. Hypocrisy, disruptive behavior, prejudice, biases, conflicts, stress effects and destructive subcultures can pose some challenges to individuals, groups and organizations. Trust and engagement hang in the balance. Relational savvy is deeply human in nature.

There is more to relational capacity than soft skills. And there is some evidence that part of our relational DNA is hard-wired. The challenge for most of us is simply this, somehow we need to match our intentions and energies in ways that bring out the best in others. This is the simple math of relational capacity. People working effectively together, in sync, as partners, as peers and colleagues, lovers and friends ... all held to account with relational capacity and competence, with tact and grace.

Think about:

- *The key areas of relational capacity*

- *How these contribute to team capacity*

- *How these complement other Talent Blocks*

- *The targets of team/relational development*

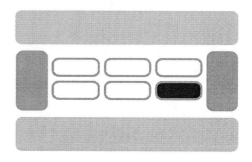

Summary Audit: Relational Capacity

Introduction

Organizations have diverse needs and requirements for Relational Capacity, and they also have different approaches to Learning and Development. The intent of this summary audit of Relational Capacity is simply to connect some themes for gauging the relevance, applications and measures that go with Relational Capacity. This audit approach can be modified to match the interests and requirements of the organization with talent development pathways that make the most sense for individuals and teams.

Relational Capacity and Competence

- ***Everyday Leadership***

  General Considerations ...
  - *situations, challenges*

  Development Considerations ...
  - *alternatives, horizons*

- ***Perspective and Attention***

  General Considerations ...
  - *situations, challenges*

  Development Considerations ...
  - *alternatives, horizons*

- ***Personal Awareness and Confidence***

  General Considerations ...
  - *situations, challenges*

  Development Considerations ...
  - *alternatives, horizons*

- ***Situational Judgment and Sense***

  General Considerations ...
  - *situations, challenges*

  Development Considerations ...
  - *alternatives, horizons*

- ***Deeper Trust and Credibility***

  General Considerations ...
  - *situations, challenges*

  Development Considerations ...
  - *alternatives, horizons*

Collective Impact and Implications

Near-Term and Long-Term Themes

Notebook

PART 3
MOVING STRATEGIC TEAMS AHEAD

Nature uses only the longest threads to weave her patterns, so that each small piece of her fabric reveals the organization of the entire tapestry.

Richard Feynman

I am a member of a team, and I rely on the team, I defer to it and sacrifice for it, because the team, not the individual, is the ultimate champion.

Mia Hamm

The future depends on what you do today.

Mahatma Gandhi

CHAPTER 09
TEAM EVOLUTION

Dynamic Teams Serve and Respond

Effective teams are powered by individuals who bring their dynamic talent to the work of making strategy happen. The combination of technical, analytic, creative, resource, solution and relational capacity is raw material for team leadership and management. Connecting these elements of talent in ways that generate value, embolden culture, serve with purpose and support progress is what dynamic team leadership and management is really all about.

Dynamic team leadership and management draws on the essential connections between the company's **Strategic Agenda** and the **Talent Blocks and Beams** of the organization, and enterprise culture.

CONSIDER:
[Shine: Brain Science, Hallowell]
[Simply Effective, Ashkenas]
[Project Team Dynamics, DiTullio]

Effective teams are quite often defined in terms of consistent focus, strong interaction, deep and broad engagement, trusted partnership and open communication. These are natural descriptors, and for most organizations, they make sense to most of us.

However, we know that different teams can serve different roles and functions, with different issues and challenges, and different support and conditions. These differences point to the importance of team leadership and management discipline. People learn to operate in team cultures and structures. They learn to connect their talent streams with the organization's Strategic Agenda. They learn to adapt and respond to changing conditions over time. They evolve.

Intentional Teams are Change Engines

Strategy is, by nature, a guide for the positive, resource-efficient, and sustainable evolution of the organization. The **Strategic Agenda** that encompasses direction, integration and execution is a framework that engages teams in the work of:

- *Generating, selecting and advancing the organization's main area of focus, and primary guiding decisions and principles*

- *Connecting and arranging the organization's body of priorities, resources, capital, systems, processes, networks, etc.*

- *Managing and accounting for the organization's actions and the impact of these actions on growth, performance and change*

In any enterprise, in any sector, conditions evolve. The mass of technical, market, political, social and economic forces drives change. Things evolve. Tensions emerge and spread and expand. Stakeholder needs change. Competitive options change. The economic prospects, risk factors and operating levers change. The stakeholders themselves change, along with requirements, behaviors and relationships. Business models and their prospects change.

Strategic Teams and Value Generation

Strategic Teams generate value in a number of ways, driving the organization's growth, performance and change. They serve to impact the revenue curve, attainable margins, resource usage, capital streams and time to break-even on new programs. Strategic Teams also serve to shape the organization's reputation, capacity and cadence of innovation, operating assets and operational excellence.

These make organizations more valuable to investors, partners, employees, suppliers and customers - their key stakeholders. They help compound the value of the organization as stakeholders want more trust in them to sustain the power to generate new economic and strategic value over time, as conditions change.

CONSIDER:
[Leading and Creating Value in the Knowledge Economy, Van Clieaf]
[Human Capital Management: Added Value Through People, Baron and Armstrong]
[Human Capital and Assets in the Networked World, Russ]

Collective Capacity

Effective teams exhibit a range of collective attributes that provide them with unique and powerful spans of capacity. We see these in everyday thought and behavior as individuals work together to address **routine processes** and **special challenges.** Teams bring forth a blend of **hard skills** and **soft skills** that is shaped further by the power and trust of:

- *Interpersonal Connections*
  - *Respect, awareness, tolerance, resolve, empathy*

- *Perspective and Confidence*
  - *Maze sense, knowledge, judgment, swamp savvy*

- *Constructive Discernment*
  - *Positive, considerate, determined, purpose-driven*

- *Exchange and Communication*
  - *Pathways, habits, routines, triggers and content*

- *Resilience and Security*
  - *Support, compassion, attention, hope and resolve*

What the best teams bring to bear is their capacity to come together, perform together, deliver results and impact, learn together and further adapt. Effective teams are dynamic in different ways, connected in different ways, nurtured in different ways. Some thrive on the tensions that shape their settings. Others thrive on performance incentives. Some are engaged in the specifics of compliance work. Others engage in breaking rules, jumping over borders, going for broke. Some are powered by the simple great joy of serving together.

Our work on **Character, Strategy and Leadership** points to some individual and team character factors that shape everyday thought and behavior in organizations. These factors are baked into cultures and subcultures. They may or may not be products of deliberate organizational Learning and Development. They may emerge with experience and duty, stress and challenges, opportunity and whim, study and deliberation.

CONSIDER:
[Collaborative Advantage, Dyer]
[Group Genius: Power of Collaboration, Sawyer]
[Cross-Silo Leadership, Casciaro, Edmondson, Jang]

Character Drivers and Themes

Broad references to character and capacity trace from studies in philosophy, the sciences, humanity, behavior, society and many other areas about what is "true and right" in culture.

Integrity
Principle, Honor, Duty, Trust, Reliability, Temperance, Uprightness, Honesty, Purity, Sincerity, Virtue, Candor, Forthrightness, Goodness, Incorruptibility, Standing

Compassion
Empathy, Selfless Caring, Humility, Service, Decency, Benevolence, Grace, Civility, Humanity, Kindness, Mercy, Sympathy, Fellowship, Charity, Consideration, Heart

Attention
Awareness, Focus, Perspective, Deliberation, Appreciation, Maze-Sense, Lenses, Consideration, Scrutiny, Thought, Absorption, Contemplation, Diligence, Curiosity,

Readiness
Discipline, Practice, Anticipation, Roadmap-Sense, Energy, Fitness, Preparation, Willingness, Fluency, Power, Handiness, Inclination, Maturity, Promptness, Prowess

Persistence
Courage, Determination, Resolve, Perseverance, Gut, Endurance, Grit, Stamina, Tenacity, Constancy, Doggedness, Pluck, Staunchness, Steadfast, Durability, Patience, Will

Stewardship
Respect, Justice, Citizenship, Collaboration, Giving, Mission, Conservancy, Faith, Maintenance, Protection, Supervision, Attention, Guardianship, Preserving, Security

Excellence
Sense of Purpose, Judgment, Navigation, Greatness, Merit, Perfection, Purity, Quality, Supremacy, Virtue, Class, Distinction, Excellence, Goodness, Superbness, Value-Driven

Obligation
Responsibility, Commitment, Accountability, Dependence, Bond, Contract, Promise, Requirement, Command, Understanding, Cause, Charge, Conscience, Engagement

These elements can mean a number of things to teams. They set the linkages between strategy, talent and culture, as well as the "why, what, who" of making strategy happen.

Collaboration and Teams

The organization's Strategic Agenda for growth, performance and change is always marked by some kind of collaboration. This could be collaboration across functions and departments, across divisions and subdivisions, across supply chain networks and systems, across technical clusters and platforms or across global country market groups. Collaboration is further set forth and explained with this simple definition:

People engaged in working together in ways that advance work that cannot, or should not, be done separately - together, with purpose and intention - for collective impact.

Collaboration is a natural synthesis of the kind of everyday thought and behavior that teams engage with and depend upon. The **culture of collaboration** is built with five themes:

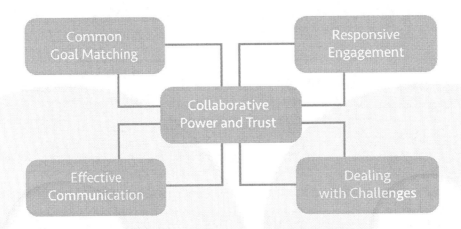

These five themes of collaboration make sense to team leadership and management. They draw from the six elements of individual and team capacity that we have explored in this FieldBook. They pivot on the incentives and constraints of teams and teamwork. They serve collectively as the **reservoir of power, energy and trust, for individuals and for teams.**

CONSIDER:
[Superminds: People and Computers Thinking Together, Malone]
[Collaboration: Building Common Ground, Hansen]
[Opening Doors to Teamwork and Collaboration, Miller and Katz]
[Big Mind: How Collective Intelligence Can Change Our World, Mulgan]
[Smart Collaboration, Gardner]

Related Challenges

Some of the broader challenges of team Learning and Development were named in earlier chapters. Now that we have the benefit of detailed coverage of six essential capacity and competence elements, some additional review of the challenges to team evolution is in order. The following are among the most common concerns:

- ***Confidence About Goals and Priorities***
  - *When the Strategic Agenda is miscued*

- ***Process Disconnects and Rules for Teamwork***
  - *When the "process swamp" kills progress*

- ***Incentives That are Contrary and/or Perverse***
  - *When motivations become wayward*

- ***Character Disconnects and Difficult Behaviors***
  - *When jerkwagons disrupt team culture*

- ***Structural Barriers to Integration/Execution***
  - *When order and arrangement block progress*

- ***Confusion About Standards and Options***
  - *When minds and souls are closed to change*

CONSIDER:
[It's the Manager, Clifton and Harter]
[Why Teams Don't Work, Robbins and Finley]
[The 17 Laws of Teamwork; Talent is Never Enough, Maxwell]

Most of us operate in a world with some uncertainty and conflict, competition and tension, ambiguity and danger. Teams and their teamwork can take a real beating when the going gets tough. Team capacity and competence can be tested by changing conditions and market shifts.

Dynamic Teams: Where and How They Learn

The conventional analysis of teams suggests that some organizations have good talent, matched to good teams, perform good work, and grow in depth and reach. However, the context for ongoing performance in any organization is subject to constant change, mixed decisions, multiple options and interwoven risks. Challenges emerge and evolve. Opportunities appear and dissolve in short order. Horizons shift, frontiers extend.

Teams work on a Dual-Dynamic pathway, considering both near-term and long-term challenges, with core business and adjacent business challenges. Market systems, technical ecosystems, economic models and social progress evolve. With the context of everything in play, we need teams that assemble, perform, adapt, advance and transform without much in the way of intervention. The pathway pushes dynamic teams:

- ***Where specific capacity and competence is built***
  - *Topical learning and action learning*

- ***Where leadership and management skills are developed***
  - *Disciplined leadership and management*

- ***Where people become agents of their Strategic Agenda***
  - *Everyday thought and behavior – for impact*

- ***Where individuals and teams have development options***
  - *Progress making, accountability, measures*

- ***Where general capacity and competence is advanced***
  - *Gaining leverage, speed, trust and value*

This is **learning by design**, to develop individuals and teams in ways that equip them to function, perform, adapt, survive and prosper, with confidence.

CONSIDER:
[Care to Lead, McGalliard]
[Teaming; Extreme Teaming, Edmondson and Harvey]
[Forming/Storming/Norming/Performing, Egolf and Chester]

Learning and Development are continuous, integrated evolutionary practices that depend on dynamic teams. **Effective teams are Learning and Development machines.**

Evolving, Morphing

Self-organizing teams, rapid-development teams, tiger teams, change management teams and seed-accelerator teams all have this Dual-Dynamic focus in common. They originate, perform and deliver with dynamic capacity and competence. They prosper with specific talent elements that breed subcultures of "Better, Smarter, Faster" practice, with better execution and better integration. Often, they transition in new forms and with new focus.

Even some "not ready for prime time" individuals and teams contribute to the advanced Learning and Development scheme of an organization. Mixing people and remixing talent, leadership and management formats, spans and structures, experience maps and action learning are part of what moves individual and team competence forward, with confidence.

CONSIDER:
[Never Stop Learning, Staats]
[Personal Learning Cloud; Responsive Open Learning Models, FoL Research, Wolf and Boomer]

Confidence Reset

When we develop and assign teams, we make known our confidence in their ability to tackle the work and make things happen. This is sometimes a leap of faith, and it is sometimes a bolder, self-fulfilling promise that people will make progress, adapt, take a few hits, recover and advance their goals. We know that **team confidence is complicated**. It depends on our perceptions of ourselves, the assignments we accept, the conditions under which we operate, the support we receive and the sense of readiness and resolve we bring to our charter.

CONSIDER:
[Daring Greatly; Dare to Lead, Brown]
[Getting Grit, Miller]
[The Confidence Code, Kay and Shipman]
[Courage: The Backbone of Leadership, Lee]

Confidence is shaped by a lot of things – neurobiology, societal influences, personal focus, experience and group interaction. What we are able to develop as individuals and as teams is what enables us to convert our everyday thought and behavior into expectations, actions and performance. Confidence evolves in this stream. **Confidence gets settled in culture**.

Team Reputation and Brand

Powerful teams earn reputations. These reputations are forged in some kind of standard of excellence. The simplest reflection of reputation-worthiness is, perhaps, a brand – a team brand. We see powerful team brands in almost every sector, the military, entertainment, corporations, social services, the performing arts, healthcare, education and unions. Teams in technology, agriculture, natural resources, supply chains, government agencies, public/private or 3P partnership also sport powerful brands, embedded in culture. We also see weak team brands across these same economic sectors, and they can become a drag on reputation and strategic value.

Reputations are important. They signal opportunity and challenge, potential and capability, relevance and connection. These are the kinds of themes that help attract, cultivate and sustain **talented people** in positive, evolving, impact-making organizations. Good teams build good employment brands. These serve to draw **talent supply chains** together for organizations as they invest in Strategic Teams.

CONSIDER:
[Treating People Well, Berman and Bernard]
[A Great Place to Work for All, Bush]
[Employer Brand Management, Mosley]
[The Talent Magnet, Evans]
[The Employee Experience, Maylett and Wride]
[Nine Lies About Work, Buckingham and Goodall]

Teams: New/Next Horizon

In broad terms, people want to work in environments where they have an opportunity to engage in truly meaningful work, where they are together with positive people in cultures that have positive team grounding. Strong, positive team cultures, shaped by a clear dedication to talent capacity and competence have a brand edge - where people develop. That brand edge is valuable, but not permanent.

Hence, we have a Learning and Development mandate of sorts, one that shapes the culture and the prerogatives of individuals and groups. Every organization has its own roadmap for developing people who become agents of making the Strategic Agenda happen. That roadmap can become a critical strategic and economic asset.

The "new/next" horizon for Strategic Teams is shaped by the work to be done as well as the organization's readiness for a more embedded kind of leadership at every level. This is true in the functional stacks of the organization, in the white space between functional stacks, and along the matrix linkages that connect functions. Strategic Teams with great talent supply chains and a sense of purpose have an obvious advantage. They have the advantage of readiness and resolve, for a world that operates in constant change mode. They have the advantage of a mindset that connects strategy, resources, culture, structure and cadence. They have the advantage of legacy.

CONSIDER:
[Designing Effective Organizations, Goold and Campbell]
[Transforming the Organization, Gouillart and Kelly]
[Rework, Fried and Hansson]

Change Leadership/Management

Strategic Teams are indeed agents of making strategy happen. That grand premise deserves to be addressed in clear view, with attention to changes that often take place with:

- **The organization's Strategic Agenda**
  - *the full picture of strategy direction*
  - *the pieces and parts of strategy integration*
  - *the everyday work of strategy execution*

- **The organization's Talent Blocks and Beams**
  - *the vertical expertise and experience beams*
  - *the horizontal awareness and behavioral beams*
  - *the primary competence and capacity blocks*

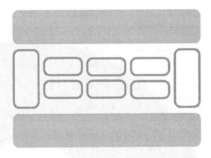

- **The organization's Cultural Agenda**
  - *the role of culture as an informant*
  - *the role of culture as a key work platform*
  - *the foundations and expressions of culture*

Change forces lurk everywhere. The marketplace, the organization, in the hearts and minds of individuals as they navigate their career tracks and their personal choices. Strategic Teams manifest their purpose, effectiveness and sustenance in a world that feeds on the forces of change.

Teams, Evolution and Focus

In the pages of **Prepared and Resolved**, we explored three general types and forms of change. These are common to most organizations as they reflect the strategic, operating and economic aspects of the enterprise as a whole:

- *Process-Level Change*
  - *often related to continuous improvement*
  - *generally shaped by Lean efforts and compliance*

- *Program and Category Change*
  - *often tied to growth and performance themes*
  - *generally shaped by integration, competitive edge*

- *Business Model Change*
  - *often related to significant changes in direction*
  - *generally shaped by significant transformation*

Settled in these types and forces of change are some unique challenges for Strategic Teams and leaders. Process-level change places some demands on efficiency and compliance, drawing hard from technical and resource Talent Blocks. Program and category change puts the pressure on teams to connect ideas and integrate new value streams; this draws heavily on analytic, creative and solution talents. Business model change is loaded with tensions that relate to strategic intent, risk and decision making. This kind of change draws hard on analytic, resources, creative and relational talent.

CONSIDER:
[The Medici Effect, Johansson]
[Strategic Change and Leadership, Wolf and Kelderhouse]
[Leading Change, Kotter]
[The Science of Successful Organizational Change, Gibbons]

Team Readiness and Evolution

Strategic Teams come together in different ways, under different conditions, with different roles, intentions and goals. Sometimes, they come together and evolve with a powerful sense of vision and readiness, and a great sense of confidence. Sometimes they are brought together with a broader mandate, untested people, experience gaps and confidence issues.

The readiness challenge for most teams is also a confidence challenge. Are we prepared, competent, open to influence and suited-up for the work to be done? Do we have our perspectives, knowledge, judgment and experience in the right place, and with the right mindset? Are we geared to taking the kind of actions that drive the kind of impact we are expected to deliver for the organization? Are we confident in teams that are stress-tested, open and adaptive, ready and resolved, geared to making strategy happen?

CHAPTER 10
FUTURE OF TEAMS

The Nature and Design of Work

Depending on the needs of stakeholders and the nature of the environment, Strategic Teams can be a powerful driver of change. The amount of change and the design of change made possible by teams will reflect many factors:

- **Systems Management and Technology**
  - *How systems interface and integrate over time*
  - *How organizations operate with system assets*

- **Organizational Structure, Governance**
  - *How organizations design themselves for results*
  - *How organizations govern their Strategic Agenda*

- **Automation, Advanced Intelligence**
  - *How cognitive and behavioral work is advanced*
  - *How people, machines, models and systems connect*

- **Education, Learning and Development**
  - *How different formats for education are built*
  - *How access to Learning and Development is enhanced*

These four elements are dynamic in nature. They reflect the forces and streams of hard content. They also reflect the many connections of human and system work, especially the who, what and how of work. They shape the work to be done by individuals and teams along cognitive, functional, emotional and behavioral lines.

CONSIDER:
[The Future of Organizations, Forrester and Leaver]
[The Future of Work, Morgan]
[The Future of Organizations; Deloitte - Volini and Andrus]
[The Project on Managing the Future of Work, Harvard Business School]

The Future of Teams, and Purpose

Strategic Teams are built with people whose collective skills and behaviors are more or less suited to the work to be done. Effective teams are formed and governed for many purposes. Their value over time and experience will reflect:

- ***Individual Readiness, Development***
  - *How self-awareness, character and attention emerge*
  - *How motivation, self-governance and confidence emerge*

- ***Collective Readiness, Learning and Development***
  - *How academic and professional learning sets the stage*
  - *How direct and indirect category experience drives maturity*

- ***Professional Competence, Safety and Experience***
  - *How social intelligence, influence and awareness emerge*
  - *How perspective, cross-engagement and appreciation emerge*

- ***Prescriptive Competence, Development***
  - *How the mix and remix of Talent Blocks is formed*
  - *How changes in the talent matrix impact Strategic Teams*

These elements are often examined in the broader soft skills conversation in the sense that they reflect behavioral and emotional factors. They also reflect cognitive and situational factors that are essential to the why, what, and who of work.

CONSIDER:
[The Attacker's Advantage, Charan]
[ISO 30414:2018 Human Capital Reporting and Standards, ISO]
[Building the Leader of the Future, Prokopeak]
[Transformational Leadership, Bass and Riggio}

Forward Development

Consider the notion of Strategic Teams as assets of the organization. The asset value of these Strategic Teams is some function of their contribution to:

- **Forward Planning**
  - *Near-term operations, long-term evolution*

- **Decision Making**
  - *Routine processes, advanced discernment*

- **Risk Management**
  - *Prevention, assessment, recovery work*

- **Problem Solving**
  - *Everyday practices, complex challenges*

Making progress with Strategic Teams is a big deal for organizations because teams are at the center of strategy, culture, resources, structure and cadence. Teams have greater or lesser value based on their engagement, competence and development. Ongoing development is what shapes the asset value of teams, directly and indirectly.

CONSIDER:
[Unlocking Leadership Mindtraps, Berger]

Strategic Teams, and Questions

The development and deployment of effective Strategic Teams is deliberate work. The methods for development are never perfect, and the routines for deployment are based on assumptions and estimates. Here are three questions that support the curation of better, smarter, faster Strategic Teams:

- **Strategy and Structure**
  - *How well do our teams reflect the direction, integration and execution aspects of our Strategic Agenda?*

- **Talent, Resources and Experience**
  - *How well does the composition, capability-maturity and collective intelligence of our people serve the purpose?*

- **Culture and Engagement**
  - *How well do our Strategic Teams assemble, perform, advance and adapt as agents of making strategy happen?*

These and other questions belong in the development conversation at different levels. Senior leadership and management teams need to have a credible view of everything in play. Strategic Team leaders and managers need to have a disciplined view of the blueprint for matching organizational systems and resources with the work to be done.

CONSIDER:
[Talent Strategy Questions Every Board Should Ask, Naerby]
[6 Questions Talent Execs Should Ask and Answer, Kaufman]

Questions: The Strategic Agenda

Does the organization's Strategic Agenda make sense to the people who are involved in making it happen? Does the organization reflect what is behind the challenges of the Strategic Agenda - the assumptions, concerns, requirements?

These are seemingly basic questions about the organization's direction, and the integration and execution of its Strategic Agenda. However, these are often more complex and dynamic than they appear. Miscues on strategy direction, the politics of strategy integration, and the constraints to execution are real and pervasive. Consider:

> ### The Strategic Agenda and the Environment
>
> *What Matters to the Curation of Value?*

> ### Connecting Strategy Direction, Integration and Execution
>
> *Where to Focus, How to Drive, What to Move?*

> ### The Strategic Agenda and the Natural Goals
>
> *What Purpose, Vision, Mission Counts?*

From start-to-finish, teams depend on the promises, objectives, inputs and concerns that are embodied in the Strategic Agenda. This is fundamental, yet for many reasons, the alignment is harder than it looks.

CONSIDER:
[Seven Strategy Questions, Simons]
[Questions that Work in Business, Finlayson]

Engaging Teams and Individuals in the Strategic Agenda

• **As an organization: What do we stand for? Where are we headed? What is our purpose? What challenges do we face?**

• **What really matters in our deck of Natural Goals, and how does any of this matter to our Strategic Teams?**

• **As Strategic Teams, what is our work to be done and how does this tie together with the rest of the enterprise?**

Questions: Talent Blocks and Beams

Does the organization's talent match up with the challenges and conditions set forth in its Strategic Agenda? Are the organization's plans for growth, performance and change in sync with its portfolio of Talent Blocks and Beams?

The common sense guidance here would focus on making sure that the organization has equipped itself with people whose competence, behavior and experience is consistent with the work to be done. For reasons known only to the Sages, this is a challenge for many, or most organizations. Consider:

The Development of Individual Talent Beams

What Drives Individual Edge, Maturity?

The Development of Specific Talent Blocks, Portfolios

What Drives Competence and Confidence?

The Development of Team/Group Talent Beams

What Drives Collective Edge, Maturity?

Talent is multifaceted. Strategic Teams with effective track records tend to be cultivated from the stock of diverse, open-to-influence people with well-blended portfolios of cognitive, functional, emotional and behavioral sense.

CONSIDER:
[Good Company, Frauenheim, Bassi, McMurrer and Costello]

Building Talent for Strategic Teams, to Make a Difference

- *As an organization, what roles do teams address in terms of cognitive, functional, emotional and behavioral capacity?*

- *What really matters in the development of teams and the curation of Talent Blocks and Beams as a whole?*

- *As Strategic Teams, what are the apparent incentives for development, and what are the constraints to development?*

Questions: The Cultural Agenda

Does the organization's Cultural Agenda serve as an informant of the Strategic Agenda? Does it provide a platform for team engagement, Learning and Development? These are the keys to enterprise culture as a working foundation, and a channel of expression.

The concerns about organizations and culture are widespread and complex in nature. These reflect values, standards, principles, habits, norms, methods and turf markers that shape everyday thought and behavior. Culture shapes motivation and engagement. It often prevails in conflicts, sometimes at the expense of decision making and problem solving. Consider:

> ## The Nature of Culture and Collective Expectations
>
> *What Informs Objectives and Work to Be Done?*

> ## The Influence of Culture on Team Development
>
> *What Shapes Readiness, Confidence and Resolve?*

> ## The Advance of Culture and Forward Capacity
>
> *What Inspires Ongoing Learning and Development?*

Culture is part mindset, part attitude, part presence, part energy, trust and the power to serve people together as agents of making strategy happen. Culture serves as a crucible for experience and a wellspring of knowledge.

CONSIDER:
[Radical Candor, Scott]
[The Culture Blueprint, Richman]

Mastering the Cultural Agenda, for Strategic Teams

- **As an organization, which cultural principles, norms and value systems are welded to the Strategic Agenda?**

- **What really matters with the engagement of people in the Strategic Agenda, with trust, energy and power?**

- **As Strategic Teams arrange themselves, develop, perform, adapt, evolve and advance, what tracks do they leave?**

Thoughts on Assessment

The sense of individual and team/group assessment divides and calibrates team effects. This FieldBook is agnostic with regard to the selection of assessment methods, but we all have our favorite methods. A practical look at **individual assessment** would consider:

- *General Cognitive Capacity and Readiness*

- *Emotional Intelligence and Social Interaction*

- *Specific Talent Block Capacity and Competence*

  - Technical
  - Analytic
  - Creative
  - Resource
  - Solution
  - Relational

- *Professional Expertise and Category Experience*

- *Adaptive Capability and Resolve to Succeed*

The assessment of collective team and group attributes, and the alignment of roles and types would consider the following as a starting point for selection and development:

- *Attitudes and Mindset for Collaboration*

- *Attention to, Adherence with Cultural Themes*

- *Capacity to Bridge and Connect Talent Blocks*

  - Sensing Differences, Serving with Purpose
  - Addressing Conflict; Difficult People, Tensions
  - Nudging and Shaping New Talent Blocks

- *Connected Expertise and Leveraged Experience*

- *Collective Accountability for Performance*

Obviously, the scale and scope of an organization can have a big weighting on the depth and breadth of assessment. These efforts have value. Further references appear on page 236.

Assessment, in Organizations
Large and Small

• *Given the nature of the organization, our challenges, and the evolving blend of strategy, talent and culture, what could we do with regard to individual assessment?*

• *Given the structure of the organization, our near-term and long-term expectations, assumptions and requirements, what could we do with team and group assessments?*

Team Reflex

The most effective Strategic Teams comprise the talent to shape, influence, drive and reset the work of making strategy happen. Their everyday practices reflect three key factors:

Team Design and Assignments	**Team Efforts and Operations**	**Team Focus and Accountability**

The powers and responsibilities that are chartered for Strategic Teams are important in a number of ways. They represent the purpose, rationale and intentions of the team, reflected in scope and design of assignments, functions and roles. Further, they serve as management and leadership disciplines, shaping accountability and tracking of performance.

Getting the right talent reflex between and among Talent Blocks and Beams is very important. Strategic Team readiness and capacity on the connections of technical, analytic, creative, resource, solution and relational talent. Drawing on the Talent Blocks and Beams of individuals and matching them for the work to be done is what makes or breaks the promise of Strategic Teams.

CONSIDER:
[Companies Should Hire Teams, Not Individuals, Finkelstein]
[Enhancing the Effectiveness of Team Science, Cooke and Hilton]

Building Talent Bridges

For many teams, building and managing the bridges between Talent Blocks is perhaps the most important leadership and management task. The characteristics and nuances of each Talent Block are unique, and we need extra attention to the interfaces that lie in the balance. Consider the challenges and constraints that go with the bridges between these particular Talent Blocks. Think about the traction, connection and balance of:

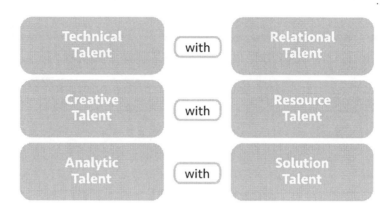

Common Concerns About Bridges

The right people, with the right talent, the wisdom to support the balance of competence, behavior, emotion and functions. The right kind of professional and personal support, with intervention, Learning and Development, trouble-shooting, cultivation, protection, guidance, tough love, practice improvement and confidence building among colleagues and stakeholders. These talent bridges are especially critical in project-based organizations.

CONSIDER:
[Match: Right Person Every Time, Erling]
[Leading Leaders, Salacuse]

Soft Skills and Hard Skills, and the Gap?

While Strategic Team competence and experience varies a great deal from place to place, from task to task, value to value, there are some common patterns of so-called soft skills and hard skills that emerge. Our Talent Bridges help address hard and soft skill gaps:

- *__Technical__, often STEM-powered people are matched with __Relational__, socially adept and interactive people to create better exchanges and cadence.*

- *__Creative__, often idea-powered people are matched with __Resource-savvy__ project management types who, together, can move the right stuff faster.*

- *__Analytic__, often data-powered people are matched with __Solution-focused__ developers and integrators who, together can make choices, move forward.*

These are examples of classic soft skill and hard skill match-ups that help make the power of Strategic Teams real. These reflect the contribution and maintenance of bridges that enable, enrich and enhance Strategic Teams at every level of the organization.

CONSIDER:
[Bridging the Soft Skills Gap, Tulgan]
[Soft Skills Like Critical Thinking in Short Supply, Davidson]
[Making a Case for Soft Skills, Lothian]
[The Case for Soft Skills in MBA Programs, Weiss]

The Matrix of Connected, Curated Talent

Depending on team design, roles, operations and focus, a matrix that connects the right competencies, the right experiences and temperament is the **Strategic Team standard.**

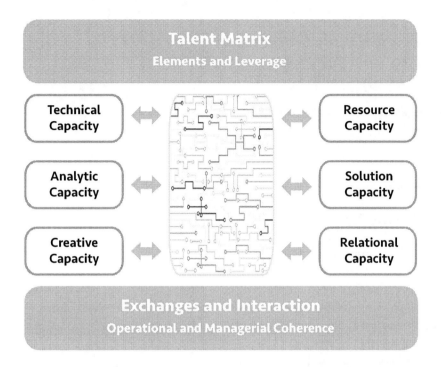

The connection between Talent Blocks are multi-directional, adaptive, multi-dimensional, subject to traction and constraint, open to personal and professional evolution, and critical for **Strategic Team coherence.** This combined with operational and managerial roles and tasks is what drives a greater standard for Strategic Teams.

CONSIDER:
[Cross-Functional Teams, Parker]
[The Cross-Functional Influence Playbook, Finerty]
[Leading Organization Design, Kesler and Kates]
[Designing Matrix Organizations that Actually Work, Galbraith]

Team Governance and Assumptions

Strategic Teams are governed with a wide range of assumptions that provide context for design, operations, focus and results. Here are some common checkpoints:

- **Assumptions About the Jobs to Be Done**
  - *The charter conditions for the team*
  - *The rationale for the work of the team*

- **Assumptions About the Criteria for Performance**
  - *The essential markers and expectations*
  - *The nature of completion, progress-making*

- **Assumptions About Resources and Appropriations**
  - *The right combination of people and assets*
  - *The connection of systems, capital, talent*

- **Assumptions About Process and Approach**
  - *Key steps, phases, inputs, stages, gates*
  - *The roadmap, the blueprint, game plans*

- **Assumptions About the Talent Portfolio**
  - *General and specific talent blocks*
  - *Known requirements and specifications*

- **Assumptions About Team Leadership/Management**
  - *Nature and intensity of leadership needed*
  - *Nature and intensity of management needed*

- **Assumptions About the "Strategic Why" of the Team**
  - *Relevance to the Strategic Agenda*
  - *Relevance of the talent assignment*

- **Assumptions About the "Strategic Who" of the Team**
  - *Individuals and team identity*
  - *Team culture and cultural expression*

These and other assumptions help individuals and teams get on track with purpose, structure, intention, markers and the broader journey of making strategy happen.

Team Departure, Journey, Destination

The roadmap for Strategic Team development and evolution is one that should have management and leadership support for the following:

- ***Departure Ramp***
  - *Understanding where individuals and teams are at present. Who they are. What they need. How they act.*
  - *Understanding with a level of transparency and relative humility, what "capacity maturity" they bring to the work.*

- ***Journey, Resources and Experience***
  - *Understanding what the road ahead brings to bear, and the nature of obstacles, detours and redirects that will occur.*
  - *Understand the necessity for preparation, scoping and scouting work, process and routing changes, improvisation.*

- ***Destination Points***
  - *Understanding the primary objective, the arrival process, the conditions of getting to what matters, what counts.*
  - *Understanding the nature of the destination as a target zone, a step to success, a placeholder for the new/next.*

CONSIDER:
[The Storyteller's Secret, Gallo]
[The Power of Story, Loehr]
[Blueprint: Evolutionary Origins of a Good Society, Christakis]
[The Leadership Development Journey, Vuhuong]
[The Leadership Journey, Burnison]
[Mobile Manager; Routes to the Executive Suite, Jennings]

Strategic Team Journal

Leonardo, Darwin, Edison and the Sherpas of DARPA all have kept track of ideas that have strategic, operational and economic process. The curation of ideas, options, insights, risk themes and pathways for navigation is logged in Strategic Team journals. These journals help connect knowledge, organize thoughts, consider transitions, and guide adaptation.

Consider these questions:

- ***What is our Strategic Team's state of departure?***

- ***What is happening on our journey of making strategy happen?***

- ***What is our Strategic Team's destination point?***

Structure and Communal Values

Strategic Teams are dependent on communal values, the prospects for working together, serving together, giving together. The prospects for collective gain, collective power, collective trust, energy and impact. The prospects for group security and safe progress-making. The prospects for serious, intentional, stretched goals and outcomes. Strategic Teams are congregate groups. Combined efforts. Shared governance. And much more.

From communal value comes a kind of organization structure that empowers and engages, connects and delivers ... across the enterprise. This is structure that:

- ***Defines and Extends Tasks and Relationships***
  - *What matters, why it matters, to whom*
- ***Frames and Assigns Roles and Responsibilities***
  - *The who, accountability and the how*
- ***Provides and Supports Practices and Standards***
  - *Platforms, foundation, roadmaps, etc ...*
- ***Gauges and Records Capacity and Progress***
  - *Progress markers, effort-to-impact notes*
- ***Frames and Navigates the Forward Horizon***
  - *Getting from near-term to long-term*

Teams are communal, greater than the individual parts. Better, smarter and faster than the solitary souls who stand as individuals without meaningful connections to Strategic Teams.

CONSIDER:
[Wired Differently, Dosch, Goulet and Finneman]
[High-Performing Teams Need Psychological Safety, Delizonna]
[Five Keys to a Successful Google Team, Rozovsky]
[Leading High-Performance Teams, Guttman]

The Future, and Beyond

Indeed, the technical, operating and economic forces of the contemporary organization will push some frontiers for Strategic Teams, as the combined, engaged, connected agents of making strategy happen. What's on the frontier?

- **Autonomous, Self-Oriented Team Development**
  - *Less hierarchy, more responsibility*

- **Advanced, Connected and Competent Strategic Teams**
  - *Greater emphasis on know-how, know-what*

- **Specialized, On-Demand Team Deployment**
  - *Readiness, productivity, speed of impact*

- **Integrated Learning and Development Resources**
  - *Built on content, access, delivery platforms*

- **Rapid-Replication Strategic Team Capacity**
  - *Suited to growth, performance, change*

- **Intramural Strategic Team Capacity Building**
  - *Practice counts in team development*

- **Rapid-Remediation and Adaptation Teams**
  - *For recovery, for risk mitigation, for ...*

- **Variations on Fantasy Team Configurations**
  - *Building team models for the future*

Each of these, in their own way, is here and now. Each of these, in their own way, beg for cultivation and translation. And there is surely more on the way.

CONSIDER:
[20 Kinds of Teams, Dewar Sloan Working Paper, Wolf and Felger]

Continuous Improvement and Development

The continuous improvement of quality, operations, services and development processes is a critical source of value creation for organizations large and small. Whether the approach is formal or less formal and situation-specific, continuous improvement in real terms depends on a combination of the elements we've defined in the page of this FieldBook.

- ### *The Strategic Agenda*
    - *Where does the continuous improvement subject, objective or target related to the focus and choices of the enterprise?*

- ### *Talent Blocks and Beams*
    - *What is the nature of the combined technical, analytic, creative, resource, solution and relational work to be done?*

- ### *The Cultural Agenda*
    - *What are the foundational and expression factors in process improvement communication, management and accountability?*

Continuous improvement targets are dependent on teams, and teams that are built for driving continuous improvement have the normal concerns about standard work, change themes, value conversion and tension. Lean and Six Sigma, check. Planned Innovation, check. And, throughout continuous improvement and performance sequences, once again, it is people in well-focused teams that make strategy happen.

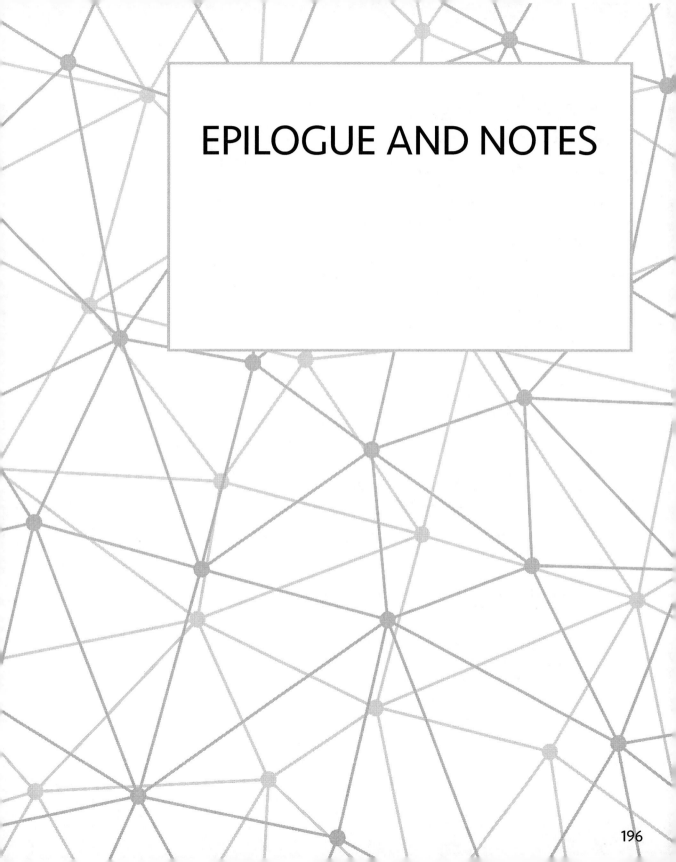

EPILOGUE AND NOTES

Themes to Consider

People make strategy happen. They do so as individuals who are capable, engaged, connected and adaptive. They do so in teams which are equipped for effective collaboration and persistent in the charters they assume. This FieldBook was developed to help shape the readiness and resilience of teams, and to press for the ongoing evolution of teams as they work to advance the Strategic Agenda of the organizations and stakeholders they serve.

Strategic Teams, built to serve with purpose.

Strategic Teams add value to organizations in many ways. They raise the potential of the enterprise. They increase the cadence of the enterprise. Strategic Teams move the needles of growth, performance and change by the force of engagement across:

- **The Strategic Agenda of the Organization**
  - *Direction, Integration, Execution*

- **The Talent Blocks and Beams, and Bridges**
  - *Competence, Experience, Confidence*

- **The Expression and Foundation of Culture**
  - *Connecting Strategy, Practices*

Strategic Teams may be assigned to work that is finite, with terminal goals and frames. They may be assigned to missions that never end, journeys that continue over the horizon and onto the next stage.

The Collective Power

The power of **Strategic Teams and Development** comes from a couple of key themes and principles. First, individuals bring a diverse portfolio of human knowledge, energy, trust, behavior, experience and discipline to the teams they gather with, and that diversity is powerful, as we see with:

- *Different points of view spark dialogue*

- *Different experiences shape ideas and criteria*

- *Different paths blend know-how, options*

- *Different temperaments ignite the cause*

- *Different mindsets allow for attention, focus*

- *Different strengths advance the collective*

- *Different energies bring new reserves*

- *Different attributes blend in the portfolio*

Effective teams communicate in unique and powerful ways. Effective teams navigate their tasks and journey with adaptive, connected, evolving and reflective new abilities that fuel action-based learning on route.

Second, individuals working together in teams have the opportunity to practice the skills that become the foundations for value creation. Different kinds of team experience shape one's ability to exchange information, provide decision support, influence problem solving, advance new concepts, anticipate risks and challenges, forge new options, and with the tensions and context that always exist, teams that stay focused on results, learn to deliver results.

The Elements

Strategy frames the organization's agenda for growth, performance and change. The hot wires that connect strategy and culture run through teams and groups of individuals whose thought and behavior is grounded in capacity and competence along important tracks …

- *Technical - knowledge, depth, scope*

- *Analytic - perspective, data sense, proof*

- *Creative - expression, expedition of ideas*

- *Resource - productive, connective, in sync*

- *Solution - alternatives, intervention*

- *Relational - communal, interpersonal*

The competence and confidence we bring forth as individuals depend on how we learn as individuals …

- *With Self-Awareness and Self-Governance*

- *Respect for and Attention to Needs of Others*

- *Attention to Priorities, What Matters, Counts*

- *Sense of Context and the Service Environment*

- *Sense of Evolution, The Road Ahead, Change*

These elements are part of the individual, group, organizational and stakeholder spans of leadership, driven at the management and governance levels.

The Domains of Teams

There are many kinds of teams. Project teams, gangs as teams, medical teams, sports teams, tech teams, executive teams, nonprofit teams, political teams, study groups and teams, maintenance crews, security teams, innovation teams, workout teams, turnaround teams, rapid-action teams, after-action teams, teams for change, teams for justice, research teams, advance teams, recovery teams, design teams, evaluation teams, construction teams, demolition teams, war fighting teams, peacemaking teams, negotiation teams, artistic teams, insight teams, red teams and forward teams.

For nearly every kind of team, there is a purpose. For nearly every kind of team there are growth, performance and change concerns. For nearly every type of team, there are Learning and Development pathways, and barriers.

Most of us are part of one or more teams that operate with a charter of some kind, with people who are more or less suited for the task, the journey, the road ahead. Most of us are capable of better efforts, smarter contributions, faster support ... of our teams. No time like the present to reset our roles, our influence, our engagement as the **leaders and agents of making strategy happen.**

CONSIDER:
[Why Pride Matters More, Katzenbach]
[The Other 90%, Cooper]
[Extraordinary Groups, Bellman and Ryan]
[Debugging Teams, Fitzpatrick and Collins-Sussman]
[Leading Teams, Hackman]
[Leading with Cultural Intelligence, Liverman]

Research Comments

The background for this FieldBook includes research from several fields including the behavioral sciences, organization development, education, neuroscience, management practice, change leadership, decision science, project management and other areas that reflect on individual and collective talent. Also reflected in this FieldBook are themes from the school of hard knocks, the lessons of individual and team experience that tend to come in complex weavings of success and failure, victory and defeat, trial and error, conflict and tension, everyday luck and the persistence of those who dare greatly, win or lose.

Personal Development Themes and Challenges

Strategic Teams and Development is the central idea we chose for this FieldBook after extensive debate and consideration. **The bottom line really is development**, and what individual and team stakeholders are willing to take on as their responsibility for ongoing, focused, team development. Consider a couple of points for **deliberate practice**:

- *Five Hours of Devotion, per Week*
  - *Most of us are busy enough in our work and our personal lives. When asked to commit five hours of extra time in professional Learning and Development, some may struggle and others will engage. Those hours, well-invested, can make a terrific difference for individuals, the Strategic Teams they populate and the organizations they work with across the journey of making strategy happen.*

- *Self-Governance plus Other-Attention*
  - *Much has been written about self-leadership and self-management, and the elements of self-awareness and social awareness. These are centered on our capacity for personal direction, our ability to organize, prioritize and sustain our professional work and our personal lives, along with our resolve to keep things moving forward, making progress no matter what. To press on, regardless.*

  - *Self-governance adds a layer of discipline, thought, perspective and regulation. Self-governance defines one's approach to situations and challenges, one's appropriation of effort, resources and time, and one's sense of personal and professional accountability. Self-governance is a big part of engagement.*

These are part of the **Strategic Team DNA**, along with the evolution of personal and professional competence, capacity and confidence. The journey has many rewards.

DEVELOPMENT NOTES

This FieldBook contains a lot of vocabulary and concepts that are not in common use for some individuals and team leaders. The purpose of the following reference is to open the boundaries a little for team discussion and development. We find that many teams generate their own version of team code and language for interaction.

This reference is part of the ongoing process of support for the development and deployment of Strategic Teams. Some of these topics and terms are the subjects of continuing education programs, webinars and Strategic Team building produced by the SC/24 Group at Dewar Sloan. We also work in collaboration with other groups to produce custom development material for specific audience and stakeholder needs.

Development Notes: Subject Matter

- **The Strategic Agenda in a Nutshell**

- **Natural Goals and the Environment**

- **Natural Goals - Expanded to Focus and Culture**

- **Dual-Dynamic Strategy**

- **Talent Redefined**

- **Maze Sense and Maze Lenses**

- **Serve, with Purpose**

- **T-Shaped Talent, Breadth and Depth**

- **Competence Redefined**

- **Strategy Engagement - Eight Elements**

Development Notes: Subject Matter

- **Teams and Risk Factors**

- **Confidence, in Confidence Alone**

- **Difficult Behaviors**

- **Processes and Rules**

- **Work-Arounds, Improvisation**

- **Execution Mindset**

- **Collaboration 202**

- **Barriers to Collaboration**

- **Culture Stream in Motion**

- **Team Ethos, DNA and Culture**

Development Notes: Subject Matter

- **Emotional Intelligence**

- **Team Design**

- **Team Emergence, Transformation**

- **Teams and Talent Casting**

- **Accountability and Teams**

- **Team Governance**

- **Objectives, Key Indicators**

- **Teams and E-Mindset**

- **Expeditionary Teams**

- **Teams and Trust**

Development Notes: Subject Matter

- **Habits and Team Effectiveness**

- **Why Teams Get Screwed-Up**

- **Teams and Stress Effects**

- **Tension Effects and Teams**

- **Teams and Compassion**

- **Communication and the Work of Teams, Part A**

- **Communication and the Work of Teams, Part B**

- **Communication and the Work of Teams, Part C**

- **Zooming-In and Zooming-Out**

- **Teams and Diversity**

Development Notes: Subject Matter

- **The Science of Teams**

- **Temperament, Teams and Character**

- **Adaptive Teams and Their Cultivation**

- **Adaptive Learning and Development**

- **Design Thinking, and More**

- **Critical Thinking, and More**

- **Team Management, Functions**

- **Self-Management, Considerations**

- **Team Leadership, Functions**

- **Self-Leadership, Considerations**

- **Team Assessment Models**

- **Enterprise Value Proposition**

The Strategic Agenda in a Nutshell

A framework for strategy leadership that engages the organization in the practical work of **making strategy happen across three main areas: direction, integration and execution**. This work is gathered between the conditions of the environment, or the marketplace and the organization, and the Natural Goals of the enterprise.

Most individuals have a general stake in the Strategic Agenda, even if they work at the front lines in more tactical and operational roles. The challenges of **strategy direction** tie to marketplace opportunities and risks, competitive conditions, economic and investment options and enterprise readiness. The challenges of **strategy integration** connect with the organization's human capital, operating models, resources, platforms, methods, agilities, economic capital, networks, practices and process assets ... and how these enable and/or constrain progress. The challenges of **strategy execution** tie to matching the right or best actions, with given conditions, to gain impact, drive results, make progress, grow advantages, adapt and sustain. The organization's Strategic Agenda is an essential platform, **a critical Learning and Development blueprint for people making strategy happen**.

Natural Goals and the Enterprise Environment

Every organization has four Natural Goals. These are defined in terms of Customer Connections, Economic Performance, Competitive Advantage and Corporate Stewardship. These are sometimes expressed in purpose, vision and mission statements, and they are connected with the realities of the environment. Natural Goals inform decision making.

Natural Goals - Expanded to Focus and Culture

Most organizations have some version of purpose, vision and mission statements that embody values and aspirations. These statements can be expressed as Natural Goals:

- **Customer Connection**
  - *Served consumers and stakeholders*

- **Economic Performance**
  - *Revenue leverage and resource leverage*

- **Comparative Advantage**
  - *Differentiation and competitive edge*

- **Corporate Stewardship**
  - *Market and social responsibility*

Strategic focus and organizational culture merge together in the expression of Natural Goals. These extend to intersections, measures and organizational challenges, and they become extensions of the organization's principles, values, standards and habits.

Dual-Dynamic Strategy

For most organizations, strategy leadership has a Dual-Dynamic focus and existence, one that deals with the organization's **paradox of contrasting ideas and concerns ...**

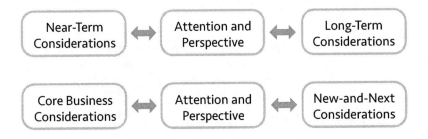

Thinking through a strategic paradox requires individuals and teams to entertain ideas, criteria, and tensions that inform planning and decision making, **with uncertainty**.

Talent Redefined

The definitions of talent range broadly, and they tend to incorporate a general collection of terms and factors that comprise the raw material for human performance ...

- **General and Specific Competence**
  - *Technical, Operational and Economic*

- **Motivation and Behavioral Energy**
  - *Based on Needs, Character and Norms*

- **Social and Network Connections**
  - *Relationships, Systems and Support*

There are many variations on this factor set, and these reflect the conditions and context of different talent forms and applications. The talent permutations of a music teacher are different from those of an epigenetic researcher. The talent factors of a 3D design hacker are different than a process auditor. The differences are powerful and beautiful, conflicting and friction-prone. Knowing the difference matters a great deal in the everyday work of teams.

Maze Sense and Maze Lenses

Individuals and teams operate with different levels of uncertainty and complexity, and the view that they have is often clouded by constraints and human drama. Maze Sense is what brings attention to things that form the context of our plans and decisions ...

- *Value Sense – character factors and foundation values*
- *Priority Sense – what matters; progress management and focus*
- *Temporal Sense – timing and use of time, adapting to time assets*
- *Power Sense – nature and use of power, influence and authority*
- *Conflict Sense – conflict, good or bad, and the management of conflict*
- *Face Sense – engagement and subject; interfaces and exchanges*
- *Opponent Sense – perspectives, differences of position, opposition*
- *Trust Sense – speed-of-trust factors, integrity and confidence*

Maze Sense is built from experience and anticipation, and building greater Maze Sense into individual and team readiness is a critical piece of **Strategic Teams and Development.**

Serve, with Purpose

People work as individuals and with teams, for some purpose. For many, that can translate to the nature of how we serve with purpose. This has cultural and structural implications.

- **Service Excellence Mindset**
  - *Founded on character, principles, covenants*

- **Service and Servant Leadership**
  - *Founded on deeper meaning, Lean practice*

- **Service in Different Perspectives**
  - *Founded on cross-disciplinary practices, habits*

- **Service Culture, DNA of Service**
  - *Founded in expectations, wisdom, perseverance*

Purpose ties to Natural Goals. Purpose ties to individual character and temperament. Purpose connects individuals and teams to the Strategic Agenda and their role in making strategy happen. **Purpose makes strategy relevant,** shaping leadership at every level.

T-Shaped Talent, Breadth and Depth

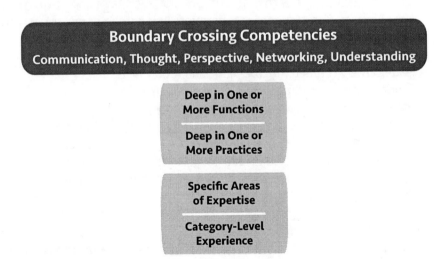

CONSIDER:
[Background: T-Academy 2018, Michigan State University; Renaissance Man, Guest]

Competence Redefined

As with the many definitions of talent, there are several key variations on the meaning and use of the term competence. For our purposes in **Strategic Teams and Development**, the main parameters of competence can be grouped as follows:

- ***Know-How***
  - *Specific and general experience, knowledge, expertise*

- ***Know-What and Know-Who***
  - *Attention and awareness of what really, really matters, and to whom*

- ***Know-Why***
  - *Conceptual and systemic oversight; context sensitivity*

Strategic leadership and influence are powered by these themes of competence, and they operate at every level of the organization, from the boardroom to the front lines.

Strategy Engagement - Eight Elements

Engagement is a term that embodies attention and commitment to something. This is a very big idea in strategy because greater strategy engagement leads to greater focus, capacity, readiness and resolve with teams that are charged with making strategy happen. **Strategy engagement is cultural and structural in nature**, and it embodies the following:

- *Intentional Learning and Discovery*
- *Commitment and Accountability*
- *Personal Talent and Enthusiasm*
- *Interpersonal Assets and Influence*
- *Systems, Order and Arrangement*
- *Discretionary Effort and Innovation*
- *Effective, Systemic Collaboration*
- *Appreciation and Human Respect*

These eight points on strategy engagement are defined in more depth in Chapter 02 of this FieldBook, with references drawn from an original article published in ***Strategy Magazine*** for the Strategy Planning Society entitled "**Strategy Engagement**" by Daniel Wolf, 2007.

Teams and Risk Factors

Anyone who has ever served on a team has some appreciation for the practical and inherent risks associated with team leadership and performance. Consider the following:

- **Risks Associated with Team Talent**
  - *Competence, motivation, connections*

- **Risks Associated with Team Charters**
  - *Attention to objectives, intended results and impact*

- **Risks Associated with Team Navigation**
  - *Attention to opportunities, constraints, alternatives*

- **Risks Associated with Team Tensions**
  - *Difficult people and difficult objectives*

Team judgment, foresight, wisdom and expertise gained through experience are the tools for managing risk and guiding the often uncertain, complex journey of making strategy happen.

CONSIDER:
[Team Conditions: Volatile, Uncertain, Complex and Ambiguous, aka VUCA]
[Five Ways Smart People Sabotage their Success, Boyes]

Confidence, in Confidence Alone

When individuals and teams are more confident, they are better, smarter and faster in the work of making strategy happen. Confidence is associated with leadership influence and:

- **Active Support and Attention**
  - *Open Development Models*
- **Relationships and Cultivation**
  - *Connections, Compassion*
- **Engagement and Encouragement**
  - *Feedback, Interventions*
- **Practice, Experience, Practice**
  - *Situations for Active Learning*

Leaders are responsible, directly and indirectly, for team confidence. The work of higher-level project and program teams places high demands on leadership and confidence building.

Difficult Behaviors

Most of us have experienced the impact of people who exhibit difficult behaviors in our personal and professional lives. These people may be psychopathic or sociopathic, they may behave badly in response to "stress effects" or conflicts. They may simply be the jerkwagon on the project review staff that holds court on planning and decision making, with or without the capacity, temperament or competence to gauge or judge, help and/or serve.

Difficult behaviors come in all flavors, and they propagate across many functions, work settings and circumstances. From a **Strategic Teams and Development** perspective, we are most likely to experience difficult behaviors and related conflict in settings that:

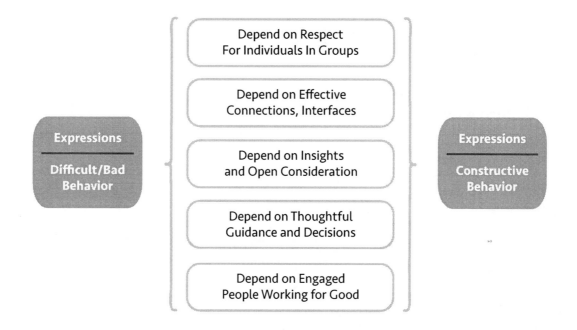

Not surprisingly, we learn about constructive behavior from experience with difficult behavior. This "education" tempers and enables us across our Talent Blocks and Beams, especially if we seek to understand others, and if we choose our teams wisely.

CONSIDER:
[Working with Difficult People, Hakim and Solomon]
[The Nature of Jerkwagons and Bad Behavior in General, Wolf and Wolf]
[The Sociopath Next Door, Stout]

Processes and Rules

For most organizations, processes are formal and informal pathways for doing routine work in a standard manner. Rules are guide posts, policy markers or stage gates that dictate what is allowable or not allowable, in some sequence or under some circumstance.

Processes and rules help bring order and arrangement to individual and team work. They provide for effectiveness and efficiency, speed and trust, quality and value, power and logic. In the broadest terms, processes and rules simplify the complex and automate the routine. These elements are positive and productive things for organizations of all stripes, unless or until they become negative things. Consider two common process concerns:

- ***Process Swamps***
    - *So much process complexity and interwoven process burden that the organization is shackled, disabled.*

- ***Policy and Rule Paralysis***
    - *Bureaucratic guidelines, although well-intended, become nasty barriers to growth, performance and change.*

CONSIDER:
[The Process Edge, Keen]
[Orbiting the Giant Hairball, MacKenzie]

Individuals and teams either prosper by, or cope with processes and rules in their core assignments and their progressions. Some open thought about the consequences of processes and rules, known and unintended, is a collateral path for team leadership and governance learning. Team work-arounds and process dodges are part of the journey.

Work-Arounds, Improvisation

From time to time, Strategic Teams are challenged to work-around a process constraint or policy obstacle. The dark side of work-arounds may reflect in risk factors and compliance concerns. The positive side of work-arounds can show in process improvement and program innovation. Improvisation is a natural act, but "good judgment" has a role.

Execution Mindset

Some people are built for strategy execution. They are prepared and resolved to get things done and master the completion of projects. The Execution Mindset considers:

- **Established Habits, Patterns and Structures**
  - *Firehouse ready, proper accommodation*

- **Constructive Attitudes About Barriers, Constraints**
  - *Practical sense of the landscape for performance*

- **Commitment to a Sense of Urgency, Based on Trust**
  - *Strong individual and team focus and ethos*

- **Personal and Interpersonal Responsibility for Results**
  - *Serious intentions, stewardship and integrity*

We also know a few things about **Execution Resistance**, the tacit and openly expressed behaviors that stifle efforts in execution. The more common types of resistance include:

- **Barriers to Information, Data Access and Knowledge**
  - *Communication flaws, inconsistent connections*

- **Barriers to Interpersonal Connection and Exchange**
  - *Coordination breakdowns and deficits in group trust*

- **Barriers Tied to Weak Discipline or Non-Compliance**
  - *Rebel activity, bad attitudes and behaviors*

- **Barriers to Team Alignment and Role Assignment**
  - *Matching people to training, projects, roles and tasks*

The Execution Mindset depends on experience, team competence and confidence, adaptive and agile behavior, a measure of curiosity, perspective, courage, influence and perseverance.

CONSIDER:
[Four Disciplines of Execution, McChesney, Covey and Huling]
[Execution: The Discipline of Getting Things Done, Bossidy and Charan]
[The Execution Premium, Kaplan and Norton]

Collaboration 202

People working together to do things that cannot be done separately, which is the essence of collaboration. The rise of "open organizations" and the advance of project teams for integration have contributed to the disciplines and cultures of effective collaboration. In this FieldBook, collaboration is examined in Chapters 02 and 09 in the context of better, smarter, faster value creation and capture, with five essential elements of collaboration:

- *Common Goal Making*

- *Effective Communication*

- *Responsive Engagement*

- *Dealing with Challenges*

- *Collaboration and Trust*

Teams are functional and social organisms that are made more or less capable in the context of these five elements. The secret sauce of high-performance teams often comes down to the behavioral incentives for, and constraints to these five elements in action. Further, the assembled Talent Blocks and Beams of individuals come together in communal fashion to advance and/or constrain effective collaboration.

Barriers to Collaboration

Working together on challenging projects is apparently harder than it looks. There are more common constraints to effective collaboration than there are incentives for effective collaboration. What gets in the way? Take a look at the following, for starters:

- *Complex and Perverse Incentives*

- *Trust, Commitment and Confidence*

- *Disjointed Processes and Practices*

- *Problems with Resource Alignment*

Effective collaboration requires **Eyes Wide Open**, and that applies to how we look at the issues that lurk with objectives, intentions, partners, competence and challenges.

Culture Stream in Motion

The culture of an organization reflects its principles, values, stakeholders, belief systems, norms, protocols, habits and other factors that influence:

- *The everyday thought and behavior of people*

- *The discernment of challenges and objectives*

- *The organization's approach to growth and change*

- *The relevance of communal, collective team effort*

Culture teaches and informs. Culture seasons and adapts with age, experience, screw-ups and challenges. Culture builds with character. Culture evolves with tensions. Culture serves as a breeder reactor for individual, team and organizational talent. Sometimes, culture protects the mothership. Sometimes, culture gets in the way of development, change and positive transformation. Sometimes, enterprise culture becomes the only driver and sustainer of comparative advantage. Culture defines and culture sustains. And, this is key, culture is a foundation for strategy and the expression of strategy.

CONSIDER:
[The Only Sustainable Edge, Hagel and Brown]
[The Resilient Enterprise, Sheffi]

Then, we have subculture. These subcultures are most often percolating in the functional, departmental and structural zones of the organization. Subcultures can be strong or neutral, perhaps quiet, maybe resistant. They can be the white space zones and tribes of the organization that hatch new ideas, grow hybrid capacity, enhance old processes and press for change. Subcultures can also be rebellious, disruptive, troublesome and distracting.

CONSIDER:
[The Culture of SC/24 Whatever: Accountability and Integration, Wolf]
[The Effect of Workplace Spirituality on Team Effectiveness, Daniel]

Team Ethos, DNA and Culture

Team culture and philosophy may be too esoteric for some, but in our experience, this idea of team ethos and DNA is very important to:

- *Recruiting and Matching the Right People to Teams*

- *Developing Individual Talent Blocks and Beams as Assets*

- *Assigning Functional Tasks and Roles to Individuals, Teams*

- *Exchanging Team Insights and Experience with Other Teams*

- *Tapping Into the Learned Readiness and Resolve of Teams*

Team ethos is the product of a set of guiding principles, personal and collective values, routines, belief systems, communal practices and governance norms that temper decision making and problem solving, risk management and forward planning.

CONSIDER:
[Corporate DNA: Learning from Life, Baskin]
[Cultural Brilliance: DNA of Organizational Excellence, Rowley]

Emotional Intelligence

The general theme of emotional intelligence reflects the confluence of self-awareness and social awareness ... how we sense and see ourselves in the context of teams and work, and how we connect with others in the social arena of working and prospering together.

Generally speaking, our maturity with emotional intelligence may battle with the maturity of our cognitive intelligence in everyday activity and performance. Emotional intelligence can also battle with functional intelligence, our approach to communication, our perspectives on problem solving, risk management and decision making. It also plays in the process of behavioral intelligence - how we interact in our everyday world.

CONSIDER:
[Emotional Intelligence, Goleman]
[Emotional Intelligence 2.0, Bradberry and Greaves]

Team Design

The idea of team design has many origins. "Choosing-Up Teams" on the sandlot or on the street has been a ritual act of matching talent to a purpose, a competitive cause, or a situation. The more sophisticated variants of team design are based on a slightly more disciplined approach that encourages:

- ***Situation Assessments***
  - *Conditions, challenges*

- ***Talent Supply Chain Access***
  - *Available and ready talent*

- ***Purpose/Vision/Mission***
  - *Strategic intentions, agenda*

- ***Objectives; Context for Success***
  - *Targeted areas of impact*

- ***Specific Talent Blocks and Beams***
  - *Prescriptive assignment*

- ***Deployment and Adaptation***
  - *Dispersion of team leadership*

- ***Action-Based Development***
  - *Learning in process, capacity*

- ***Team Design Governance***
  - *Cumulative practices*

There are many kinds of teams, and the wise and ambitious design of teams is something to consider before, during and after team assignments, and throughout the journey.

CONSIDER:
[Teaming; Extreme Teaming, Edmondson and Harvey]
[The Wisdom of Teams, Katzenbach and Smith]

Team Emergence, Transformation

More often than not, the character and capacity of teams gets developed in the course of project assignments, through experience. Individuals bring certain Talent Blocks and Beams to the party and then, through the activities of the project or team assignment, they learn to apply their unique competencies to the tasks at hand. That is team emergence.

Sometimes it seems easy, and sometimes that learning and emergence process is just a good old lesson from Hell, with work from Hell and people from Hell. The so-called crucible of experience is where we forge our Talent Blocks and Beams in practice, and for most of us, this crucible of experience is the essential "why" for the emergence of high-performance, high-persistence teams that grow into great enterprise assets. Team emergence is growth.

CONSIDER:
[Hiring for Attitude, Murphy]
[Reinventing Talent Management, Lawler]
[Connectivity in the Human Age, Mercer Global Talent Trends]

Teams and Talent Casting

Effective teams can be assigned in a number of ways, with and without specific disciplines and casting rules. The research behind this FieldBook strongly suggests a casting approach that takes into account the broader talent situation. Matched with other issues, especially the cultural and strategic frame:

- ***Casting rules need to match the Strategic Agenda***
  - *Purpose, intention, stretch considerations*

- ***Casting processes need to be credible, focused on talent***
  - *Criteria, method, evaluation sequences*

- ***Casting should be open to "surprise" opportunities***
  - *Experience matched with emergent talent*

Talent casting is also a factor in our assessments of organizational culture and the culture of readiness and resolve. The culture of accountability. The culture of curiosity and exploration. The culture of expertise and knowledge and strategic insight - the culture of resilience and perseverance. When we cast people into roles, tasks and relationships, we're obligated to measure-up with culture, making sure that competence, trust and confidence are served.

Accountability and Teams

One of the many facets of human engagement is accountability. Individuals and teams take responsibility for their efforts, their practices and their results, the cause-and-effect stream of metrics, working with diligence, bringing out the best in others and ...

- **Accountability for Knowing What's Up, What Matters**
  - *Context, circumstances, conditions*

- **Accountability for Matching Efforts, Practices, Results**
  - *Understanding the roadmap, cause-and-effect*

- **Accountability for Dealing with Distractions, Problems**
  - *Expecting the speed bumps; readiness and response*

- **Accountability for Getting People Engaged, for Results**
  - *Managing the journey, staying on the goal*

Others look at a kind of Dual-Dynamic accountability that has contact and engagement with two ideas at once. The near-term/long-term and the core/new-and-next differences.

This Dual-Dynamic view of accountability reflects in the work of teams engaged in business growth and change, compliance, adaptation or resettlement.

CONSIDER:
[Propeller: Change and Accountability, Corbridge, Jones, Hickman, Smith]

Team Governance

Somebody has to set the rules. Somebody has to clarify the objectives. Somebody has to keep things on track. Somebody has to assure compliance, solve problems, help the struggling, serve the budget masters, keep the peace and order, drive the wagons, fuel the engines, settle the conflicts, make the revisions, deal with set-backs, rally the troops, sound the retreat, nurture the newbies, engage the sages, and otherwise guide what matters and how the team adapts in the work of making strategy happen. This is team governance.

Team Governance involves power and trust, support and choices. Team governance is formal and informal, structural and situational, political and social, cultural and administrative.

CONSIDER:
[Boards and Strategy, Wolf]
[Innovation Governance, Deschamps and Nelson]
[What is IT Governance? Lindros]
[The Key to a Better Board: Team Dynamics, Charas]

Objectives, Key Indicators

Many organizations work with key performance indicators, process variables and objective result measures to guide individual and team activity. These markers are best when they connect expectations, behaviors and performance in a cause-and-effect manner, with:

- ***Purposeful Connections to the Strategic Agenda***
  - *With a powerful "why" with each goal*

- ***Intentional Connections to Teams and Development***
  - *What is relevant? How are things aligned?*

- ***Practical Accountability, Rules Where Appropriate***
  - *What matters? How is progress measured?*

- ***Balanced with Enterprise Culture and Intentions***
  - *With due consideration for values, norms*

CONSIDER:
[Hard Goals, Murphy]
[Objectives and Key Results, Niven and Lamorte]
[Radical Focus, Wodtke]

Teams and E-Mindset

Of relevance to many organizations is the approach to entrepreneurial activity that is built into the so-called **E-Mindset**, also known as the **entrepreneurial mindset**. This includes:

- *Self-Governance and Direction*

- *Personal Order and Arrangement*

- *Active Views on Risk Management*

- *Adaptive Discipline, Readiness*

- *Applied Critical Thinking Practice*

- *Environmental Sense and Insight*

- *Resource Savvy and Appropriation*

- *Curiosity, Persistence, Courage*

This has obvious cultural and talent implications, and it ties back to ideas that define compliance, integration and discovery subcultures.

CONSIDER:
[The Entrepreneur Mind, Johnson]
[The Entrepreneurial Mindset, McGrath and MacMillan]

Expeditionary Teams

Organizations may assign teams to explore frontiers, evaluate risk factors, scope-out markets, gather insights, map technology, assess supply chains, review value streams, examine networks, gauge the enemy, enlist partners and a host of other considerations. These endeavors can shape team Learning and Development, as well as team value.

CONSIDER:
[Competing for the Future, Prahalad and Hamel]

Teams and Trust

Trust me. That simple request which individuals and teams make of each other is loaded with cognitive and behaviors themes.

- *Cognitive themes* like confidence in another person's competence, skills, performance, resolve. We trust in the content provided by the other person.

- *Behavioral themes* like emotional contact, warmth, compassion, friendship, affection, temperament. We trust in the connection with have with others.

Trust is part character, part of a subject in which we become invested in the confident expectation of something, some effort, outcome, action, impact, responsibility for results. Trust is rewarded. Trust is sometimes broken, sometimes suspended, sometimes recovered, sometimes protected in the process of formal and informal governance.

CONSIDER:
[Elements of Influence, Bacon]

Habits and Team Effectiveness

James Clear, author of **Atomic Habits**, suggests that habits are elements of a system that connects knowledge, emotions, behaviors, relationships and the way we operate as individuals and teams. Understanding habits is fundamental. Consider:

- *The Nature of Habits, the Power of Habits*

- *Tracking, Seeking, Mapping, Sensing of Habits*

- *The Aggregation and Leverage of Powerful Habits*

The bigger "habit constellation" of positive action, professional beliefs, personal behaviors, and forward roadmaps drive making strategy happen. Habits empower and enable teams.

CONSIDER:
[The Power of Habit, Duhigg]
[Atomic Habits, Clear]
[The Seven Habits of Highly Effective People, Covey]

Why Teams Get Screwed-Up

Beyond the obvious screw-up factors of team communications - tied to trust, information, patience, interaction and focus, there are many explanations for **why teams don't work**...

- *Confused, Perverse Objectives*

- *Unresolved Roles and Responsibilities*

- *Lack of Team or Group Governance*

- *Inadequate Data, Data Competence*

- *Cultural Malaise on Scope, Urgency*

- *Perverse Incentives and Markers*

There are many, many other reasons why teams don't work but they tend to collapse into the above, and these tend to merge with a series of cultural and leadership concerns.

CONSIDER:
[Don't BS Yourself, Taffer]
[The E-Myth Revisited, Gerber]
[The Knowing-Doing Gap, Pfeffer and Sutton]

Teams and Stress Effects

Individuals and teams are often challenged by **stress effects**, impacting their capacity to function and interface with others. Stress effects can impact the work to be done:

- *People Focus Too Much on Constraints, Barriers*

- *They Distort Reality, Misread Actual Conditions*

- *They Misread Common Signals and Core Messages*

- *They Get Obsessed with Risks and Vulnerabilities*

The antidote to stress effects begins with a disciplined check on reality and alternatives. Better information, more conversation, more perspective, more discernment.

Tension Effects and Teams

Tension effects are essential concerns that can impact a team or organization in both negative and positive terms:

- *Concerns about roles, intentions, priorities*

- *Concerns about standards of behavior, intentions*

- *Concerns about norms, practices, habits, views*

- *Concerns about competence and courage*

Team members and leaders may emerge as tension-avoiders or, in some cases, tension adapters. Both can serve a purpose on the team, depending on the quest or need for harmony, and the quest or need for intervention and/or disruption.

CONSIDER:
[Reconcilable Differences, Markova and McArthur]
[Crucial Conversations, Patterson, Grenny, McMillan and Switzler]

Teams and Compassion

Effective teams are generally better equipped with authentic attention to the human needs and concerns of stakeholders. They care for one another and themselves, the people and purposes they serve. They are mindful, open to concerns, thoughtful about the context and content of work, and helpful. And below, more for consideration:

- *Compassion extends to the development of individuals*

- *Compassion is expressed as part of the work stream, value stream*

- *Compassion is balanced by hard goals and mission command*

- *Compassion is part of entrepreneurial team interest and ideals*

Teams are small communities of interest, armed with intentions, taught through stories and narratives, powered by emotions as well as the rational acts and processes of making strategy happen. Teams work with a cause, and that cause is a key driver of compassion.

Communication and the Work of Teams, Part A

Effective communication is a big deal for strategic teams and influencers. While we could look at communication as a normal part of **Relational Competence**, there is much more to the equation. Here is a basic picture of team communication and what's involved:

When team stakeholders suggest that communication problems are lurking in their midst, something in this mix is off. The challenges tied to sending and receiving, content and message streams, and intervening factors are always in play.

CONSIDER:
[Communication: The Cleveland Clinic Way, Boissy and Gilligan]
[Intercultural Competence, Lustig and Koester]
[Power Listening, Ferrari]

Communication and the Work of Teams, Part B

Research by the **MIT Human Dynamics Lab** and research generated by others who study team function and performance point to four key factors in team communication value:

- **Energy of Exchange**
  - *Everyone communicates and interacts*

- **Levels of Engagement**
  - *Everyone interacts across lines and frames*

- **Ranges of Exploration**
  - *Everyone looks at undiscovered paths, ideas*

- **Nature of Extensions**
  - *Everyone connects, vertical and horizontal*

The idea is that team communication cannot be an optional or elective act. Communication is a normative value that is expected, deserved and managed, and part of team DNA.

CONSIDER:
[The New Science of Building Great Teams, Pentland]

Communication and the Work of Teams, Part C

Breakdowns in communication can be caused by interpersonal conflict, cultural issues and differences, perspectives, experiences and situational concerns. Gender and generational factors, structural factors, task/role and relationship factors all play a role in communication breakdowns. The mechanics of listening, the power of narratives and the management of content all play a role in the effectiveness of individual and team communication.

CONSIDER:
[That's What She Said, Lipman]
[Reclaiming Conversation, Turkle]
[Conversational Intelligence: Great Leaders Build Trust, Glaser]

Zooming-In and Zooming-Out

Teams depend on the capacity of individual members and leaders to shift their lenses and perspectives. This enables greater insight and it invites shared learning and discernment. It supports a Dual-Dynamic view of strategy and it helps the organization navigate.

- ***Zooming-In to Gather a Closer Look at the Details***
  - *Shaped by personal relationships, content influencers*
  - *Shaped by situational elements and specific contexts*

- ***Zooming-Out to Gather a Broader Look at the Big Picture***
  - *Shaped by general observations about the environment*
  - *Shaped by the cause-and-effect factors that circulate*

CONSIDER:
[Thinking For a Change, Gelb]
[Thinking Fast and Slow, Kahneman]

Teams and Diversity

Generally speaking, diversity is a basic attribute of effective teams and the work they generate. But there is more to the Diversity Factor than appears. The ongoing research behind **Strategic Teams and Development** points to four areas of diversity:

- *Social and Cultural Diversity*

- *Cognitive and Intellectual Diversity*

- *Gender and Generational Diversity*

- *Personal and Identity Diversity*

Diversity can help drive perspective, judgment, ideas, reference points and speed of thought. Diversity can also drive tension, barriers, conflict, discord and distrust. Better, smarter, faster teams figure this out, to their advantage.

CONSIDER:
[Decision Making and Diversity Matters, Apfelbaum]

The Science of Teams

Effective teams may appear out of the darkness, but more likely, they are designed to function and perform with the benefit of science. Academic, military, research and enterprise teams that are tapping into the science of teams are focusing on:

- *The social aspects of team interaction*

- *The dynamic of team leadership, support*

- *The effects of trust, confidence, exchange, power*

- *The nature of conflict, rewards and purpose*

Many interdisciplinary teams require higher-order capabilities that are shaped by the science of connecting, learning and executing. This subject is unfolding, and it will become even more relevant across the range of team designs in both complex and simple organizations.

CONSIDER:
[The Strength in Numbers: Team Science, Bozeman and Youtie]
[The New Science of Building Great Teams, Pentland]
[Collaboration and Team Science, Bennett, Gadlin and Marchand]
[The Science of Team Science, Stokols, Hall, Taylor, Moser]
[The Science of Teams in the Military, Goodwin, Blacksmith and Coats]
[SciTS Conference, Science of Team Science 2019]

Temperament, Teams and Character

Individuals and teams come together in organizations in a relatively broad mix of social temperaments. These temperaments tend to reflect behavioral tendencies as well as personalities, and sometimes personality disorders. Positive and contented people with high ideals and aspirations. Calculating and hard goal people with rational dispositions. Artistic and expressive people with open drawing boards. Rule-bound people with big compliance interests. Systems-driven people with integrative, collaborative tendencies. The list goes on and on. The most effective teams attend wisely and cleverly to their temperament issues.

CONSIDER:
[Turning Team Performance Inside Out, Nash]
[The I in TEAM: Accelerating Performance, Gerke and Berens]

Adaptive Teams and Their Cultivation

Teams operate, learn and develop in their assignments and through their functions. How they adapt, when they adapt and who does the adaptive work of engagement is all part of the process. The research suggests that individuals and teams adapt to challenges, roles and functions on the basis of four common team learning and adaptability factors:

Common Team Adaptability Factors

There are natural barriers to adaptation based on human attachment and cohesion issues, organization structures, cultural norms and how teams are designed, built, cultivated and assessed. The most effective teams tend to be adaptive by design.

Adaptive Learning and Development

Across the fields of formal and informal education, the subject of adaptive Learning and Development is evolving. People adapt with cognitive approaches and patterns. They adapt with regard to conditions and challenges. They adapt to learning methods with exposure to practice and applications. They adapt to content, structure and context of a host of Learning and Development experiences and streams of developmental exposure.

CONSIDER:
[Adaptive Technologies for Learning and Work Environments, Lazzaro]
[Adaptive Capacity and Project Teams, Edmondson and Metcalf]
[Emergence, Johnson]

Design Thinking, and More

The general term, **Design Thinking**, has been used to describe the constructs and pathways of **human-centered design and development work**. The essentials of Design Thinking are:

- *Cultivation of Needs; Idea Management*

- *Visual Interpretation of Idea Flow and Logics*

- *Exploration of Potential; Expression in Briefs*

- *Provisional Settings for Experimentation and Service*

- *Construction of Narratives, Prototypes, Propositions*

- *Demonstration, Collaboration, Influence and More*

Throughout **Strategic Teams and Development**, the concepts associated with ideas in Design Thinking tap into and across the Talent Blocks and Beams we cover in this FieldBook.

CONSIDER:
[The Design of Business, Martin]
[Innovation by Design, Lockwood and Papke]
[Design Thinking, Cross]

Critical Thinking, and More

A broadly used term, **critical thinking** means the capacity to generate sound answers to important questions, to make good decisions with logical arguments, reasoning and facts. To work with data and premises, background knowledge, operating insight and a blend of curiosity, wonder, open-minded exploration, memory, influence and evaluation. Critical thinking blends all the elements of our Talent Blocks and Beams model. To comprehend, interpret, engage facts, render concepts, and build conclusions ... this is the critical focus.

CONSIDER:
[Critical Thinking, Chatfield]
[The Organized Mind, Levitin]
[Predictably Irrational: The Hidden Forces That Shape Our Decisions, Ariely]
[World Without Mind, Foer]

Team Management, Functions

In the pages of **Prepared and Resolved**, we went to great lengths to explain the nature of management and leadership, and their differences. For reference, **team management** is defined in terms of **what management really does** … in practical, everyday terms:

- *Provides Discipline*

- *Orders and Arranges*

- *Disperses Resources*

- *Supports Practices*

- *Supports Processes*

- *Shapes Targets, Goals*

- *Sets Proper Boundaries*

- *Encourages Quality*

- *Manages Risk Factors*

- *Provides Information*

CONSIDER:
[What Really Works: Sustained Business Success, Nohria, Joyce, Roberson]
[Scaling Up Excellence, Sutton and Rao]

Self-Management, Considerations

Self-management begins with personal awareness and carries the same general themes and functions as entitled above. The emphasis on self-management is built on the basis of personal direction, organization and motivation.

Team Leadership, Functions

Team leadership, for the purposes of this FieldBook, goes along as a complement of team management as an element in team effectiveness. The **key elements of leadership** are part of the work that:

- *Shapes Perspectives*

- *Frames Value, Principles*

- *Engages and Inspires*

- *Forges Connections*

- *Engages Relationships*

- *Provides Foresight*

- *Clarifies Options, Focus*

- *Encourages Thought*

- *Encourages Character*

- *Shares and Exchanges*

CONSIDER:
[Act Like a Leader, Think Like a Leader, Ibarra]
[The Captain Class, The Hidden Force That Creates the World's Greatest Teams, Walker]
[Leadership Can Be Taught, Parks]

Self-Leadership, Considerations

Self-leadership builds on personal insights and introspection and carries through on the general terms and functions outlined above. The emphasis on self-leadership is made on the basis of personal aspirations, navigation and commitment.

Team Assessment Models

There are several avenues for the assessment of team readiness, function, advantage, roles, tasks relationships, energy, trust, power, conflict, process, chemistry and performance. Some teams are geared to thrive with just the right mix of people whose Talent Blocks and Beams align well with the work to be done. Others are built to engage, adapt, develop and advance as part of their charter, part of subculture, and in the context of the work to be done.

While team challenges, processes and structures vary a great deal, some consideration of classical and evolutionary team roles is appropriate. These may include:

- **The Role of Organizer, Arranger, Director**
    - *Getting the Trains to Run on Time*
- **The Role of Expert, Thought Leader, Specialist**
    - *Providing Knowledge and Perspective*
- **The Role of Integrator, Networker, Improviser**
    - *Bringing Critical Pieces and Parts Together*
- **The Role of Navigator, Pathfinder, Executor**
    - *Matching Progress-Making with Destination*
- **The Role of Operator, Task Producer, Checker**
    - *Getting the Work to Be Done - Completed*

Dynamic, self-directed teams have variable values and approaches to team role and task governance. Roles evolve as Talent Blocks and Beams adapt.

CONSIDER:
[Team Performance Assessment and Measurement, Brannick, Salas and Prince]
[Team Effectiveness in Complex Organizations, Salas, Goodwin and Burke]
[Developmental Sequence in Small Groups, Tuckman]
[Management Teams: Why They Succeed or Fail, Belbin]
[Virtuoso Teams, Fischer and Boynton]
[The Four Tendencies: Personality Profiles, Rubin]
[The Team Descriptive Index, Lee, Koopman, Hollenbeck, Wang and Lanaj]
[Team Quotient: High-Performance Leadership Teams, Gerber]

Enterprise Value Proposition

An important aspect of strategy engagement is the value proposition that is used to define, convey and enforce the essential elements of the organization's Strategic Agenda. This idea serves to bind the organization's Talent Blocks and Beams, and the Cultural Agenda expoused and expressed in everyday thought and behavior.

The enterprise value proposition defines:

- ***The Promise of the Customer Experience***
  - *Reflecting real customer requirements*
  - *Reflecting key points of market difference*

- ***The Capacity to Deliver on that Promise ...***
  - *Reflecting technical and operating assets*
  - *Reflecting service levels and working assets*

- ***The Consequences for Stakeholder Groups***
  - *Reflecting the interests of the organization*
  - *Reflecting the interests of the marketplace*

The enterprise value proposition speaks to the employees, customers, investors, partners and suppliers, as principal stakeholders with a set of expectations. These help connect the Natural Goals of the organization with the challenges of the marketplace.

CONSIDER:
[Delivering Profitable Value, Lanning]
[The Value Proposition - Strategic Purpose, Wolf]
[Value Proposition - Catalyst for Innovation, Lindič and DaSilva]

Other Teams and Development Themes

Other Teams and Development Themes

About the Author

Daniel Wolf advises executives and governance leaders on the direction, integration and execution of strategy. For more than 25 years he has served in the trenches with talented people who are the agents of making strategy happen. In his corporate career, Dan was part of many team adventures in product development, worldwide planning and integration, market planning, business development, operations and resource management.

Working with the strategy and governance practice he co-founded, Dewar Sloan, Dan has been influential in resetting the work of strategy leadership into a team effort, for people serving as agents of making strategy happen. His earlier book, **Prepared and Resolved**, serves as a foundation for much of the work defined in **Strategic Teams and Development**. The work with his book **Boards and Strategy** follows many of these core themes.

Strategic teams have been a professional interest to Dan and his group at Dewar Sloan since day one. Dewar Sloan has served hundreds of organizations, and most share this general observation ... talented people, working effectively together to advance the needs of stakeholders is what cranks performance and assures progress with regard to:

- Organic growth and development, new products and services, new customers and markets, new channels and systems

- Business innovation, exploration and acceleration, integration and advancement, maturity and replacement

- Business change and evolution, system adaptation and response in structure, culture, resources, strategy

These and other areas are the natural home, the natural focus, the natural theme of **Strategic Teams and Development**.

That's our story.

Grateful Reflections

Many people have contributed to the content, expression, premises and context of this FieldBook. The author is grateful for the ideas and arguments of a huge roster, but specific thanks go to Dave Thompson, Karen Weaks, Tom Palmer, Buddy Bernbaum, Janet Ziegler, David Fosdick, Jayne Huyser, Wilbur Beall, Donna Wise, Chris Wollam, Kathleen Root, CEH, Steph Swartzendruber, Mack Renfro, Becky Kelderhouse, Bill Hammerstein, Albert Serianni, Earl Parker, Frank Bacon, James Gritter, Eugene Jennings, David Harris, Germane Hoover and a bigger, endless list of professional friends and colleagues whose great insights, experience, acumen and wisdom dot these pages.

In addition, a long cast of research interns and contributors have added their reflections and findings to the mix. Caroline White, Charlie Zhou, Jordan Stokes, Amy Brassell, Chris Wollam, Kellyn Sanders, Colleen Mrazek, Pat Seyferth, Kelly Blair, Natalie Wallace, and Carolyn Fasulo have served in the collection of research elements, design elements and related content.

Now, for the real story of **Strategic Teams and Development.** For at least a decade, Julie Anstandig Wolf has been the high priestess of getting this book from a bunch of disconnected ideas and noise, to a working premise, to a construction site with all the attendant language of a construction site, and to a resource that organizations can engage and prosper with. The "quiet one" on the Strategic Team is often the toughest critic and the smartest coach, the servant leader, the snack getter and the greatest partner. Really.

Professional Services and Programs

The SC/24 Team at Dewar Sloan produces and delivers a range of support and advisory resources for Strategic Teams. In addition to this Fieldbook, we have powerful vertical programs that address strategy, talent and culture themes. We also collaborate with other professional service providers in the development and support of executive education programs, planning programs, portfolio management models, and governance programs.

The **SC/24 Program at Dewar Sloan** offers a number of program resources that complement **Strategic Teams and Development**:

- *Leadership and management retreats that deal with strategic planning, decision making, project planning*

- *Special interest group workshops that speak to challenges and opportunities for growth and change, evolution*

- *SC/24 program briefs, an extensive series of subject matter notes and micro-learning materials for Strategic Teams*

- **Strategic Teams and Development** *blueprints for use in advanced corporate learning and engagement institutes*

- *Keynote programs for educational, institutional, trade group, professional society and corporate planning meetings*

- *Webinars:* **Strategic Teams and Development***, focused on key issues in enterprise strategy, talent and culture.*

For senior executive teams and boards, Dewar Sloan also provides support for leadership transitions, M&A integration, organic growth programs, organization change, innovation progress and a host of custom Learning and Development programs.

Research Papers and Protocol

Ongoing research by our SC/24 Team provides updates and comments on several areas of interest for **Strategic Teams and Development** followers. Briefing Papers for each of these areas are available upon request, supported with semi-annual notes on trends and issues.

Contact dboomer@dewarsloan.com.

The Strategic Agenda:
The Framework for Growth, Performance and Change

Talent Blocks and Beams:
Understanding and Integrated Approach to Talent Development

The Cultural Agenda:
The Framework for Culture as a Foundation and Expression for Strategy

INDEX